C000271371

THE ART OF KIND AND FLOWING RELATIONSHIPS

A PRACTICAL GUIDE TO DEAL WITH YOUR DIFFERENCES AND CREATE HAPPY RELATIONSHIPS THAT LAST

Nicholas Haines

First Edition published 2020
Copyright © Nicholas Haines 2020
The right of Nicholas Haines to be identified as the author of this work has been asserted by
him in accordance with the Copyright, Designs and Patents Act 1988.

All rights reserved. No part of this book may be reproduced by any mechanical,
photographic, or electronic process, nor may it be stored in a retrieval system,
transmitted, or otherwise be copied for public or private use other than for fair
use as brief quotations embodied in articles and reviews without prior written
permission of the publisher and copyright holder.

Cover design: Charlotte Mouncey
Cover images: © Nicholas Haines
Authors Photograph by kind permission of © Nicholas Haines

Printed in Great Britain by TJ International Ltd

A CIP catalogue record for this book is available
from the British Library
ISBN 978-1-8380365-0-8

Dedicated to my love, Sue

With my deep and forever love

Table of Contents

PART 4: The Artist's Toolbox   111

PREFACE

When I was five years old my mother became very ill. As a result I spent over a year in different family homes, moving every few months. In each new home I was shown extreme kindness and care at one of the most confusing and difficult times in my life. Even though I was very fortunate, unlike many people in this situation, I still became a rather anxious child and hyper-vigilant as to how to fit in. All hidden behind a jolly exterior.

In my adult life, as well as having a happy marriage and three wonderful children, I had the privilege of spending thirty-five years practising and teaching Traditional Chinese Medicine. I recently calculated that over that time I conducted over 50,000 one-on-one consultations. The majority of these consultations included either a request for some relationship support or a discussion about what was working well - or going badly - in their life and relationships.

The content in this book is the result of a lifetime of obsessively observing how we interact or get on, over 50,000 consultations and a wonderful and deeply loving marriage and family life.

ACKNOWLEDGEMENTS

I'd like to thank all my patients over the last thirty-five years for guiding me and trusting me, and for helping me form and develop these ideas in the real world. Without you this book would not exist.

I'd also like to thank and acknowledge Matthew Newnham, co-founder of the Five Institute, for his great skill, talent and relentless commitment to pull this content from me. And of course Janet Carter, also of the Five Institute, for constantly pushing me to write this book and for her conversations, thoughts and dedication to kindness. Thank you both.

Very special thanks go to the remarkable Jacqui Lamont, whose sensitivity and commitment to exploring and experimenting with Conscious Questions allowed me to develop them way beyond what I ever thought was possible.

I'd also like to thank Rúna, Mia, Bitta, Monique, Aloise, Stuart, Jacqueline, Jo, Mica and Kay for your love and for pushing me to do more and be more. For my network of colleagues and dear friends, who are too many to mention, for inspiring me to shift my thinking and for providing me with a vision of how to burn brightly in the world. You know who you are, and I love you dearly.

To Carole and Lisa, thank you for the laughter and for making my writing space sparkle.

Special thanks go to my adorable little sister Emily, whose magical ability to spot my typos and mistakes allowed me to relax and enjoy the whole process of writing this book.

I also want to thank and give my appreciation to Catherine Cousins and everyone at 2QT Limited (Publishing) for their sterling work in getting this book ready and to print.

To the hundreds of people who actively and passionately share The Vitality Test and the thousands upon thousands of people who take it, I thank you. As I do the members of our Five Institute community – online and offline – who constantly encourage us, share what we do, always turn up, and make this a wonderful place to be.

Finally, I would like to shine love and light on my family, those of you who are with us and those of you who are no longer here. My dearly departed parents, my lovely wife Sue, my sons Lewis, Benjamin and Elliot and their partners. My three sisters, Charlotte, Lucy and Emily, and my brother Hal and all our extended family, including my stepmother Rosie and my parents-in-law Jim and Ann. You have all been my rock and my reason, and your brilliance and skill in how to have relationships that are kind and flow shine through in this book. Thank you all.

INTRODUCTION

This book and its supporting content have been written for anyone who wants to have healthier, happier and more empowering relationships in their life – relationships that are kind and that flow. The relationships could be with loved ones, friends, your children, family members or even yourself. Although this content isn't specifically designed to help build teams or support your working relationships, you'll find plenty of useful content here for doing just that, and if you need more, then please email me at nick@fiveinstitute.com

The secret sauce within this material comes from the Five Energies, which is one of the things that separate this content from all the other currently available material on building better relationships. We hope you find this content supportive, insightful and valuable in all your relationships and throughout your life. (If you've arrived here without taking The Vitality Test you can take it via this link: www.fiveinstitute.com/rb, which will take you to our website.)

This book is split into four parts, each of which can be read separately and independently of the others. However, they are designed to complement one another and add extra dimensions of understanding, brilliance and problem-solving to any relationship issues you have.

PART 1: SETTING THE SCENE

The three chapters contained in Part 1 set the scene for us. In Chapter 1 I'll share the six main challenges our relationships have to deal with. After that we'll move on to Chapter 2 and explore the nature of flow in our relationships and what happens when friction and stagnation start to build up. Then we'll end Part 1 with Chapter 3, which gently pulls apart the idea that we should treat others the way we want to be treated.

PART 2: THE ANCIENT CHINESE ARE HERE TO HELP

The two chapters in Part 2 focus on the Five Energies and your Vitality Test results, and explore the gifts and the challenges that each Energy brings to our relationships. This starts with Chapter 4, where I give you an overview for each of the Five Energies, followed by Chapter 5, where we look at the secret to living with each Energy and explore the ins and outs of day-to-day life with each Energy.

PART 3: THE FIVE RELATIONSHIP KEYS

The eight chapters in Part 3 take you through the five relationship keys. They are what we consider to be the five most important things you need to do to unlock or to reach the full potential in your relationships.

PART 4: THE ARTIST'S TOOLBOX

In the final part of this book, The Artist's Toolbox, we give you a wonderful set of reference guides, and look at the ten different combinations (pairings) of the energies. Each one explores what works well within each pairing and flags up some of the most common challenges to watch out for. This combination of energies could be seen in a friendship, a work relationship, between a couple, or within the parent/mentor role with a child.

PART 1
Setting the Scene

'You only live once, but if you do it right, once is enough.'
—*Mae West*

The three chapters contained in Part 1 set the scene for us.

In Chapter 1 I'll share the six main challenges our relationships have to deal with. After that we'll move on to Chapter 2 and explore the nature of flow in our relationships and what happens when friction and stagnation start to build up. Then we'll end Part 1 with Chapter 3, which gently pulls apart the idea that we should treat others the way we want to be treated.

1

Know Your Foe Like a Friend

'Once we accept our limits,
we go beyond them.'
—Albert Einstein

When our relationships work well they bring enormous joy, happiness and meaning to our lives. And when they don't they can lead to some of the most painful, troubling and difficult times we will ever experience. The state of our relationships has a massive influence on how we feel, function and experience the world. So it's imperative to have the best understanding and tools available to support you and your relationships.

Let's start by briefly explore some of the difficulties our relationships have to deal with – what we're up against – and then move on to our solutions.

The Six Main Challenges Our Relationships Have to Deal With

1. We're all different and complex and see the world through our own lens.

'The good life is one inspired by love and guided by knowledge.'
—Bertrand Russell

One of the greatest challenges within our relationships is that we all see and experience the world in a different way. We can share the same experience, hear the same words, be in the same place, and yet have a completely different interpretation of what we've just experienced, seen or heard.

And, if that's not complicated enough, we all have different responses to the situation as well. Not just based on what we think we've just experienced but based on who we are as people.

Relationships are complicated because we are complicated and we are all different.

By the time you've finished this book you'll know yourself and others like never before. The Vitality Test and the Five Energies are simple and yet profound ways of making sense of why we do what we do and what drives us all. Challenge Number 1 will be a thing of the past.

2. We don't always have the best relationship with ourselves.

'Over the years, I've interviewed thousands of people, and I would say that the root of every dysfunction I've ever encountered, every problem, has been some sense of a lacking self-value or of self-worth.'
—Oprah Winfrey

Suffice to say that it's very difficult to have a good relationship with someone else if you don't have a good relationship with yourself.

One of the aims of this book is for you to have a better relationship with yourself and, dare I say, to love and value yourself a little bit more.

3. Preformed thinking, listening and responding.

'Things yet unknown will change the way you think.'
—*Toba Beta, Master of Stupidity*

Have you ever had a conversation before a conversation? This is where you've rehearsed in your mind what they say, then what you say, and, ultimately, how the conversation ends.

That's an example of preformed thinking, listening and responding, which we all do to a lesser or greater extent. Preformed thinking, listening and responding is very common and can be a useful strategy for rehearsing your position or for getting clearer on what you're going to say and how you're going to say it. The challenge is that preformed thinking, listening and responding can also lead to more fixed positions and a preformed conflict.

Another example of preformed thinking, listening and responding, which we'll explore more in Part 2, is when our Energy, history or current state of mind predetermines our way of thinking, listening and responding. For example, you might have had a bad time at work one day, where you become increasingly annoyed by stupid behaviour and things not being done well. Then, when you arrive home, your thinking, your listening and your responding are all in that preformed state. Which may – or may not – be helpful when you're dealing with a teenager or anyone else you encounter.

And then there is the preformed thinking, listening and responding that come as a result of putting people into boxes. This is classifying someone based on some aspect of who they are, where they come from, or some other arbitrary or made-up fact about them.

The bottom line is that there are many reasons for preformed thinking, listening and responding, all of which end up as a challenge that our relationships have to deal with.

4. Life gets in the way.

'I am very busy, life is very busy, and I was, I think,
a somewhat lazy friend. I love them, I know they love
me, but I didn't make much of an effort.'
—*Jane Green*

It's very hard for most of us to isolate ourselves and our relationships from the activities, stresses and strains of everyday life. Money worries, time pressures and exhaustion all get in the way of our relationships. Not to mention work, hobbies, dreams, our health and everything else we've got going on.

Life has many joys, distractions and stresses that will have an impact on your relationships, all of which have to be navigated. The content within this book and its supporting material are designed to help you navigate through life in a smooth and delightful way.

5. Being in a permanent state of change and evolution.

'Change is inevitable. Change is constant.'
—*Benjamin Disraeli*

Within any long-term relationship, the one thing we can be certain of is that the person we started the relationship with will change over time. As humans we are in a constant state of change and growth with our ideas, our attitudes, and with the way we see the world. Time and experience change us on many levels, and this means that we have to constantly adjust to the new reality of who we are in a relationship with.

And then there are the hormonal and developmental changes that take place, both within us and in those we have relationships with.

In a nutshell… just when you get to know someone, they change at some level.

Although change is inevitable and part of life it doesn't have to be an issue. Within this book and in our work at the Five Institute we have ample ways of supporting you to flow and to adjust through change.

6. Sabotage, testing and the past.

'We are not held back by the love we didn't receive in the past, but by the love we're not extending in the present.'
—*Marianne Williamson*

Most of us have stuff going on because of who we are, or because of what's happened to us in the past. This can be beneficial for our relationships and at times a challenge for them. If you've already taken The Vitality Test or have previously engaged with any of our work at the Five Institute, you'll have heard us talk about testing. Testing is when we create some sort of test to find the answer to a question that each Energy drives us to ask over and over again.

For example, Fire Energy drives us to find the answer to the question about whether we're loved and appreciated or not. So Fire Energy testing might be to do something to make it harder to love us, just to find out if we're unconditionally loved or not.

As we delve deeper into the Energies we'll see more and more how the Energies in our Vitality Test profile can sabotage or put stress on our relationships as a result of testing.

MOVING ON

In the next chapter of this book we're going to explore what happens when friction, stagnation and stuckness exist in our relationship and start to explore the power of flexibility and flow.

2

Understanding Flexibility and Flow

'Your task is not to seek for love, but merely to seek and find all the barriers within yourself that you have built against it.'

—*Rumi*

Flow and Getting Stuck in a Hard Place

The easiest way to understand the nature and importance of flexibility and flow within our relationships is to look at what happens when it's not present: when we're in a place of friction, stagnation and stuckness.

First of all, let's define what we mean by friction, stagnation and stuckness within our relationships. Then we will explore the seven signs that you should look out for as indicators that you're in that place or heading in that direction.

To a certain extent, friction, stagnation and stuckness are all the same thing, just at varying degrees of severity.

Friction

When you see two people who aren't getting on, there's friction between them. Any ability to glide or flow smoothly past each other in terms of ideas, views or opinions has disappeared. There's a resistance, which could be passive or more overtly aggressive.

It might be irritability or anger, a cutting remark, an unkind comment or, in some cases, a complete lack of communication. You'll often also see friction in their physical ability to move around each other too. They'll be some bumping into each other or almost purposefully an obstruction of each other's path and getting in each other's way.

Stagnation and stuckness often arrive when any areas of friction aren't being dealt with or have been there for a long period of time.

Stagnation and Stuckness

Stagnation and stuckness can be less obvious and perhaps less painful than friction, but as a state it can often be more damaging in the long term as it starts to destroy or interfere with our deeper sense of who we are, or of what is possible.

When we're stagnant or stuck in our relationship there is often an inability to accept something or let it drop. There's a bogged down, heavy and unyielding or fixed quality to what we say, do or how we behave with each other, and the lightness and flow have gone. Or there could be a lack of interaction between you, interspersed by intense emotions or reactions. When we reach a state of complete stuckness we're often at an impasse when one person is forced to reluctantly yield, or the horns stay locked.

Let's look at the seven signs of friction, stagnation and stuckness next to give you more of an idea of what these states look and feel like. Remember that they are along a spectrum and, in reality, can blend into each other.

Seven Signs of Friction, Stagnation and Stuckness

1. Tension, irritability and anger.

These, in a way, are the most common or more obvious states to see or experience when we have friction, stagnation or stuckness in our relationships. It is, however, worth mentioning here that anyone with a reasonably high percentage of Wood Energy (roughly about twenty-five per cent and upwards) will be more prone to having irritability and anger issues as a response to even the slightest friction, stagnation and stuckness, and that issue could be that they don't express or show any anger.

2. Depression, low moods, being withdrawn.

In Chinese medicine it's recognised that one of the causes of depression is when irritability and anger as a force start to travel inwards instead of being expressed outwardly. So, for some people, their response to friction, stagnation or stuckness would be to become more withdrawn rather than show any outward signs such as anger and irritability.

3. Lack of communication or a burst of talking.

I always think of this sign of friction, stagnation and stuckness as being similar to a tap when there's an interruption to the flow of water. Nothing happens and then splutter-splutter, and it all comes pouring out.

I remember twenty years ago giving a lovely lady an acupuncture treatment for a painful foot, which I treated by using an acupuncture point that is well known for moving stuck energy. After the treatment she went home happy and pain-free, but that night she woke up with a jolt and started to tell her husband everything she had wanted to say to him for the last fifteen years.

Oh boy, did I have some explaining to do.

4. Tiredness and fatigue.

When our energy is stuck, then tiredness and fatigue are really common to see as a symptom. It's almost as if having energy that is stuck is like not having any energy at all. When we sit for too long or don't move enough we can feel sluggish and tired. Then, when we get up and have a walk, we feel less tired all of a sudden. All we've done there is to move our energy, not increase it.

So, when our energy is stagnant or stuck, we feel tired and fatigued.

5. Game-playing, teasing or winding up.

I think we've all witnessed children when they are trapped together or restricted in some way. They start to push boundaries, wind each other up, and start to play games with us or each other. Adults are no different.

When there's friction, stagnation or stuckness in our relationships then we'll often see some sort of games being played, or teasing or winding up as a response.

6. Increased or decreased sex drive.

More often than not having good and joyful sex moves our energy, particularly if an orgasm is involved. It's a release of some sort.

That being said, we're all very different when it comes to what makes us want to have sex in the first place or what puts us off.

Some people, when they feel stuck or their energy is stagnant, want to have sex to get that release, while for others it's the last thing on their mind.

The difference in our individual sex drive in general, and whether stuck or stagnant energy increases or decreases our desire for sex, is a really common area of stress conflict within our intimate relationships.

Sharing this idea of friction, stagnation and stuckness increasing or decreasing our sex drive was a really helpful concept to many couples in my acupuncture practice, as it increased their understanding of each other and helped to reduce further tension and stress.

7. Pain or discomfort.

If you bang your knee or knock your arm the most common response is to rub it to make it feel better. Rubbing, massaging or creating some movement helps many types of low-level pain because it moves the energy in the area. This movement of energy is the basis of acupuncture theory in the treatment of both physical and emotional pain.

In our relationships (and in life) when energy is stagnant or stuck then we commonly feel pain as a symptom, which for some people could manifest physically and for others as emotional pain. As a rule of thumb, the more stagnation and stuckness there is, the worse the pain will be.

Mixing and Matching and Patterns of Accumulation

In reality when there is friction, stagnation and stuckness in our lives we tend to have a mixture of all these signs and symptoms at various levels of intensity. Generally, when I was in practice, I'd look for patterns of accumulation – where someone is almost collecting or amassing these signs or symptoms in their life as the lack of flow isn't being addressed.

So consider your life and relationships and think... Are you accumulating signs and symptoms of friction, stagnation and stuckness?

And if you are, don't worry. That's what we're looking to address within this book.

Your Next Chapter

In the final and very short chapter within Part 1 of this book, we're going to very briefly explore a rule of conduct found in many religions and cultures, that's as daft as daft can be.

But before we do that, I just want to mention one thing...

The Danger of Being Resilient and Adaptable

In many areas of life, it's good to be resilient and adaptable. In fact it's often promoted as a way to be. To lean in, knuckle down and tough it out. However, being resilient and adaptable in terms of friction, stagnation and stuckness isn't a great idea, for two main reasons.

1. Friction, stagnation and stuckness are just symptoms.

The signs and symptoms of friction, stagnation and stuckness that are showing up in your life are telling you that something needs to be addressed. So ignoring them or digging deep into your resilience to cope with them won't be doing you any favours in the long term. It's far better to tackle the underlying cause, rather than just being resilient and adaptable to the symptoms.

2. Prolonged friction, stagnation and stuckness can lead to health issues and illness.

In the area of health, often the more serious or troublesome problems arise as a result of some system or process getting stuck or obstructed. Very rarely do we run out of energy to do something. It's nearly always a build-up or an accumulation of something. So, to stay in good health, we want to encourage flow and movement and to address the underlying causes of friction, stagnation and stuckness.

3

The Madness of a Genius Idea

'I've learned that people will forget what you said, people will forget what you did, but people will never forget how you made them feel.'
—*Maya Angelou*

The Golden Rule

> # The Golden Rule:
> *Treat others the way*
> *You wanted to be treated.*

The Golden Rule is the principle of treating others as you'd like to be treated. It is a general truth or rule of conduct found in many religions and cultures. And, in terms of our relationships, it's a fundamentally and deeply flawed idea. Why on earth would you treat someone as you'd like to be treated? Surely you should treat them as they'd like to be treated.

Can you imagine if that happened?

22

Just imagine what life and the world would be like if you treated other people in a way that they wished to be treated, and they treated you in the way that you wished to be treated.

Remember the first challenge that we have within our relationships? We're all different and complex, and we all see the world through our own lens. Well, this highlights the importance of knowing and understanding other people and treating them in a way that suits them and not you.

So how do we understand and know what suits other people, or what are their fundamental requirements in life?

Here's where we bring in the amazing Five Energies and start Part 2 of our journey.

PART 2

The Ancient Chinese Are Here to Help

'Study the past, if you would divine the future.'
—*Confucius*

In the next two chapters, which form Part 2 of this book, we'll start to explore the Five Energies as a way of understanding and explaining why we are as we are in life and in our relationships. And, from that place of deeper understanding, we'll move on to the practical application of the Five Energies in all our relationships.

Background to the Five Energies

In China, about 2,500 years ago, there was an astounding time when great thinkers like Confucius, Zou Yan and the Taoist philosopher Laozi offered a fresh perspective on the art of living, relationships and how to understand ourselves and the world around us.

It was during this remarkable time, which became known as the Hundred Schools of Thought, that the Chinese philosopher Zou Yan proposed that everyone is born with a specific Energy makeup, a unique blueprint, composed of Five Energies: Water, Wood, Fire, Earth and Metal.

These are what we measure when you take The Vitality Test.

The specific balance of these Five Energies determines how you see the world or respond to any situation you find yourself in. It is because we all have different Energy types that two children or adults can have exactly the same experience, but nevertheless interpret it in radically different ways.

The Five Energies give us a framework or map for navigating the complexity of human nature and behaviour. They are a powerful way of understanding yourself and others and they have the ability to support you in your relationships and in daily life.

If you've arrived here and haven't taken The Vitality Test you can take it free of charge via this link: www.fiveinstitute.com/rb, which will take you to our website.

4

The Vitality Test and the Five Energies

*'One of the most beautiful qualities of true friendship
is to understand and to be understood.'*
—Lucius Annaeus Seneca

When someone first takes The Vitality Test – and we get on to the subject of relationships – the most common question we are asked is...

'Which combination of energies gets along the best?'

And our answer is always the same:

'There are advantages and disadvantages to any combination of energies. It's really more about whether or not you care for or love that person, and your ability to be open and kind, that decides if the relationship is going to work or not.'

So don't worry if you're comparing Vitality Test profiles and you see that you and someone in a key relationship to you has a similar profile to yours, or one that is the complete opposite. Both are a hundred per cent fine.

The real secret is to understand the person and how they see and respond to the world, and from that place to keep the relationship flowing and moving forward. That path allows any combination of energies to have the most wonderful relationship of mutual respect, harmony and empowerment. When that happens, both people get to be themselves and bring out the best in each other.

What we have given you already

In the report that accompanied your Vitality Test profile, we included a comprehensive guide exploring two of your most dominant energies.

In this book we've gone one step further and given you access to a comprehensive guide to all Five Energies.

Use this link to access this specially dedicated webpage: www.fiveinstitute.com/full-set which you will find on our website.

And in Part 4 of this book, The Artist's Toolbox, we give you ten different combinations (pairings) of energies. We'll explore what works well within each pairing and some of the most common challenges or what to watch out for. This combination of energies could be seen in a friendship, a work relationship, between a couple or within the parent/mentor role with a child.

Having said that, we don't suggest you go to either of those places just yet, unless you're someone who needs or likes to have lots of detailed information before you can start.

Instead, we suggest that you start by focusing on a simple overview for each Energy, which is in the following section, and that you pay most attention to the Big Question which, you may remember, is the key question (one per Energy) that our Energies ask over and over again.

The Big Question is one of the most important things you need to know about and to consider within your relationships. Doing this will help increase understanding, reduce stress and allow a state of flow and harmony to exist. So, if you focus on the Big Questions for you and the people in your key relationships, you will get the best results, and more quickly and easily.

As you read the following overviews, see if you can spot someone you know.

Remember, we're each a blend of all Five Energies, often with just one or two being more dominant. As a result, we're often attempting to answer more than one Big Question.

Terminology

It's also worth saying at this stage a little bit about the terminology we use, and what we're looking at when we describe someone as having a certain one of the Five Energies.

One of the important things to recognise about your Vitality Test profile is that it isn't a label or designed to box you in. What we identify when someone takes The Vitality Test is a fluid pattern of the Five Energies that are interacting together to make you who you are. You're unique, especially if you consider that nobody has ever had your exact life.

At times, in this book and in other material, we use the term Water type or Wood type, etc. What we are really referring to are the qualities that come from that Energy rather than to a type of person. Even if someone has, for example, seventy-five per cent of Metal Energy in their Vitality Test profile, and that's a really high percentage of one Energy, they still have twenty-five per cent of the other energies in varying percentages. And so they can't be described as a Metal type. Who they are is a balance of all the energies, and they just happen to have a single dominant Energy.

So you'll see us use type as a way of describing an Energy rather than a person. Think about yourself as having certain types of Energy rather than being an Energy type. Or that your Energy type is your unique blend of all the energies.

Getting to know the Five Energies

We're going to start with a brief overview for each of the Five Energies so you can start to get a sense of the energies you haven't yet met.

Water Energy Overview

Their Big Question is, 'Am I safe or is it safe?'

Water as an Energy can make us risk-averse in some areas and risk-takers in other areas. As such, those with a dominance of Water Energy tend to always be looking towards the future and what might happen. Someone with a lot of Water Energy will often have an interest in sustainability or the long-term impact of something. Generally, they like to have time to reflect on what has happened or what will happen. They often have a big purpose and/or want to help others find theirs as well as the ability to dig deeper and stick something out. Anyone with a dominance of Water Energy in their profile will often have a natural authority and can be a great thinker.

Wood Energy Overview

Their Big Question is, 'Am I free or am I trapped?'

As a result, they hate feeling boxed in or trapped. Wood Energy makes people very flexible, but don't be fooled: push them too far and they will snap. They have lots of ideas and can have some issues with finishing things off. They can be rebels and rule-breakers and like to challenge conventional thinking, but they really hate it when others break their rules. Anyone with a lot of Wood Energy will hate injustice and will take a stand against it, even if it means they lose out. They can be chaotic at times, or very ordered and controlling. Their challenge is finding the balance.

Fire Energy Overview

Their Big Question is, 'Am I loved or do I bring joy?'

From that place they are brilliant at making people feel comfortable and appreciated. They love to have fun, to make people laugh and to share stories. They can, however, be inappropriate with what they say if they are nervous or overexcited. It's important to recognise with a Fire type that just because they are laughing it doesn't mean they are always OK or happy.

People with a lot of Fire Energy are often wonderful connectors and love to share connections and help people, although they can promise too much or can take on too much, especially if they are excited about something. A common big issue with Fire types is that they can burn out if they don't learn to be selective and say no.

Earth Energy Overview

Their Big Question is, 'Do I understand and am I understood?'

As a result, they love to understand and be understood and make the time to listen. Often you'll find them in caring, listening or teaching roles. Their challenge is that they can chew things over or get bogged down when they don't understand something or waste lots of time as they try to work something out. People with a lot of Earth Energy can have issues around food, and can overeat or undereat when under stress. They are inclusive, community-driven or family-driven, and they like people to get along well together. Someone with an abundance of Earth Energy will often be a naturally caring, supportive person who constantly observes what happens and how other people feel in any given situation.

Metal Energy Overview

Their Big Question is, 'What is missing or incomplete?'

As a result, they will be brilliant at identifying what's missing or what still needs to be done. Anyone with a dominance of Metal Energy will love quality and simplicity. They will often use numbers to assess what is there or what is missing, or to measure the value of something. Metal Energy drives them to deplore waste, to like to have things completed and on time and ideally to be done in the simplest way possible. They can get caught up in high levels of perfection, which can lead to overwork and isolation. They have an amazing ability to step back and distance themselves from a situation, which can be misunderstood as not caring, which isn't true. They often need to be alone to work something out and can feel vulnerable and exposed if you suddenly put them in the spotlight.

So there we have it: an overview for each of the Five Energies.

Did you spot the qualities and traits of someone you know, or even of yourself?

It's worth repeating again: you don't need to remember anything more than the Big Question for each Energy at this stage. That's quite enough. And, of course, I have described each Energy in isolation, whereas in reality we all manifest as a blend of the Energies we have in our profile.

At this stage of the book you have two choices…

1. Read in Chapter 5 about the dominant Energy or energies of the person you want to get to know and understand better. You can also read about your own energies in that chapter too, as this book is about you having a better relationship with yourself too.

2. Skip that, and go straight to Part 3 of this book, The Five Relationship Keys, where we'll start to explore the practical application of the Five Energies in your relationships. Remember, you can always come back to the content in the section entitled The Secret to Living with Each Energy at any time, or use it as a reference guide.

5

The Secret to Living with Each Energy

'Your task is not to seek for love, but merely to seek and find all the barriers within yourself that you have built against it.'

—*Rumi*

Here is a simple set of guidelines to help you live with each Energy. Remember again that the person you're living with may well have a combination of a number of energies. So, although this content is split into each Energy, we're rarely defined by one single Energy.

You'll also find at the end of this chapter a few final thoughts about the energies, which are well worth reading at some stage.

Living with Water Energy

Their Big Question is, 'Am I or is it safe?'

Water Energy drives us to constantly look for the risk in any situation or take risks in order to find the answer to their Big Question, 'Am I safe or is it safe?'

As a result of living with someone with dominant or a strong amount of Water Energy, you could find yourself reassuring someone who comes from a place of fear or living with someone who needs to be protected from themselves, as they take what seems like one unnecessary risk after the other (some of this could be playing out over long periods of time).

They are always looking backwards or towards the future and what might happen.

Water types as an Energy can spend a lot of time either looking backwards or forwards, and as a result those with a dominance of that Energy can miss out on the joy and magic of this moment or be approaching life from a theoretical point of view.

So, if you're living with anyone with lots of Water Energy in their profile, it might be helpful from time to time to remind them that now is a great place to be and that life is safe and worth fully engaging with, as well as taking advantage of their talents to look at and secure your future.

They often have an interest in sustainability or the long-term impact of something.

Don't think you can play a short game if you're sharing your life with someone with lots of Water Energy in their profile. They'll love to remind you of the impact of your actions and often the importance of safety and protecting your future. That's just who they are.

They like to have time to reflect on what has happened or what will happen.

When you live with someone with lots of Water Energy it's important to give them space and time to reflect and think things over. Trying to rush them or persuade them to take action quickly will result in a much slower decision-making process and you'll just be putting them under stress.

They often have a big purpose and or want to help others find theirs.

It's important for Water types to have a purpose behind what they do or know the reason behind what they are being asked to do. Saying, 'Because I say so,' to a Water Energy child just won't wash.

With a Water Energy adult, they will only be able to stick at a job or a task without meaning for so long before they start to starve and dry up inside. Purpose and meaning is their lifeblood.

They have an ability to dig deep and stick something out.

Regardless of whether or not this digging deep and working long hours is due to testing their stamina (or perhaps it is because they are on a bigger mission to save the world) it can result in you having to watch a Water type push themselves way beyond what's normal. Sometimes it's our responsibility as a partner, a parent or a friend of someone with lots of Water Energy to protect them from themselves by advising them to rest and take a recovery break.

They often have a natural authority.

Water dominant profiles can get used to having lots of authority, and as a result they can struggle at home when they might be seen as a mere mortal, which can get tricky.

So choose your battles wisely, especially if they are adamant about a really big safety issue. At some point they'll be right, and then you're in a sticky 'I told you so' place.

Living with Wood Energy

Their Big Question is, 'Am I free or am I trapped?'

How to handle someone with Wood Energy? Give them their freedom, or a sense that they have more choices than they actually do. Either way they'll be happy. Push them the other way or box them in and you'll see a side that may not always be as rational as you'd like or expect.

They can be very flexible, but don't push them too far or they will snap.

One advantage of living with someone with lots of Wood Energy in their profile is that they are normally very flexible, adaptable and easy-going by nature, especially when they're relaxed and in control. The challenges start when their life goes less smoothly, or they feel under pressure or out of control. Here you'll see a different side to them. They can be snappy, controlling, inflexible and downright stubborn. The secret is to keep them moving and active with a sense of freedom. Then you'll have a happy bunny in your life.

They have lots of ideas and love anything new.

When you live with someone with lots of Wood Energy, be prepared for a thousand and one ideas. Your challenge is that they might not all be good ideas and they may well arrive in a burst of frantic, unstoppable activity. Plus expect the latest gadget or idea to arrive in the house or be the centre of attention way ahead of anyone else. Wood types are archetypal early adopters.

They can be rebels or challenge conventional thinking.

Don't expect to witness or live a life of compliance and sticking to the rules if you're sharing your time with someone with lots of Wood Energy. That's unless it's the rules they have decided are important, and then they have to be strictly adhered to.

They hate feeling boxed in or trapped.

I'd suggest that you don't arrange a surprise caving holiday. Anyone with a Vitality Test profile full of Wood Energy hates the thought of being confined in small spaces, and that goes for being boxed in or trapped within a conversation or situation. Give them lots of freedom to manoeuvre and you'll bring out the best in them.

They can have too many ideas and so don't get things finished.

I hate to break it to you, but you may not be in a relationship with a completer-finisher.

They hate injustice and will take a stand against it, even if it means they lose out.

You won't always see logic at play when Wood Energy is in town. They'll naturally take a stand against what they see as an injustice or as unfair. However, when they're incensed, any sense of what's good for them or you can go right out of the window as they fight the good fight.

They can create chaos or bring order.

Wood Energy gives anyone an amazing capacity to create chaos and a mess in an instant, and at the same time have the ability to tidy and sort out an overwhelming mess with an unstoppable determination. Your challenge is that you're not always going to have the right action at the right time.

They like a plan but don't always stick to it.

Anyone with strong Wood Energy in their profile loves a good plan, but when it comes to sticking to it, or keeping to the planned time, there can be issues. Or you could be living with a version of Wood Energy who is rather fixed on their plan, and who is highly stressed that you're not keeping to what they have decided. The secret is to go with the flow in the moment, and when the time has passed and their stress has reduced have a quiet word about how you feel.

Living with Fire Energy

Their Big Question is, 'Am I loved or do I bring joy?'

The secret to the heart of anyone with plenty of Fire Energy and their happiness is to tell them they are loved and appreciated. And as they tend to forget that, tell them frequently and repeatedly. If their Fire Energy doesn't feel appreciated or loved, it's as if you've taken away the very fuel that keeps them burning brightly and at their best. Also, it's also important to acknowledge their love directed towards you, as it comes from a special and precious place and they are expecting a response.

They are passionate, excitable people but can take on too much.

Passion and excitement are trademarks of anyone with a dominance of Fire Energy, but those hot emotions can lead to their downfall as they often take on too much and possibly go into burnout territory.

If you're sharing your life with someone like that, I'd suggest that you have a loving conversation every now and again about the art of saying no, and that you watch the amount of time they spend on social media.

They love to talk but sometimes don't listen as much as they should.

I guess that's something you're going to have to live with, although with training they can get better, especially if they know it's difficult for you. The bottom line is they won't want to make you unhappy or feel unappreciated. So, when they remember, you'll get a word in.

They are very good at making people feel comfortable.

Most people quickly warm to anyone with lots of Fire Energy, as long as they aren't too over the top or too overexcited, which can be a struggle or just plain annoying. Think how quickly you felt comfortable when you first met your Fire type, and felt like you'd known them forever.

Just because they are laughing doesn't mean they are OK or happy.

This is a big one to watch. Just because you're hearing a laugh or seeing a smile it doesn't mean they are OK and feeling happy. It could be just the opposite. The thing you need to understand about Fire Energy is that it makes us highly sensitive to emotions. It's part of its brilliance. So be mindful and observant when someone with a dominance of Fire Energy is joking around when they're in a tough situation. It may be their defence or their way of dealing with feelings that are too intense to cope with.

They can be inappropriate with what they say if they are nervous or overexcited.

Be prepared to cringe, be annoyed or even shocked by someone's Fire Energy when they are nervous, overexcited or on a quest to make people laugh. Humour is a fine line and Fire Energy makes us cross it at times.

They are wonderful connectors and love to share connections.

They will have more great/best friends than any other Energy and are also happy to connect people together. The secret to repaying that act of generosity is to make sure you sing their praises and show your appreciation when you acknowledge that the connection has been made.

They love to have fun and make people happy.

Sometimes you'll find that people with lots of Fire Energy will make people laugh at their own expense or you're being subjected to a barrage of jokes, impersonations or one-liners by them. Those with lots of Fire Energy have to have space and an opportunity to bring love, joy and laughter to the world. Without that they struggle with their own happiness and purpose. So create that space and time, and enjoy.

Ultimately, if you've got someone with a lot of Fire Energy in your life you've got someone who wants to make you truly happy and have a life that's full of fun and enjoyment.

How good is that?

Living with Earth Energy

Their Big Question is, 'Do I understand and am I understood?'

If someone with an abundance of Earth Energy doesn't understand what's happening or if they think they've been misunderstood it creates an enormous amount of distress and stress for them, which is hard to fully understand if you haven't got much Earth Energy yourself. So bear with them and give that extra bit of time to meet that need. Having said that, you may reach a point at which you have to help them accept and reach an understanding that the situation, person or whatever it is they are struggling with can't be fully understood, and that's how it is. In a way, that's the understanding.

They will always offer help but often don't ask for it.

It's important to check in with your Earthy companion to find out if they need any help, and don't assume that, because they say no, it's true. As well as not asking for help, they can be very bad at accepting help when it's offered. A way to solve this conundrum is to make it clear that it would mean a lot to you to help them, and then you've switched it round to them supporting you.

They can easily move from supporting into sacrifice.

There is a fine line between supporting someone and being in a place of sacrifice, and in many a case they readily overlap. This area is a challenge for Earth Energy types, and as such those around that Energy need to be aware of that possibility, and protect, advise and support them in this area. Sacrifice is occasionally a necessary boundary we all have to cross, but it shouldn't become a way of life.

They are naturally caring, kind and supporting.

Those with lots of Earth in their Vitality Test profile are in their element and in a very natural place when they are caring for and supporting others. It's in their DNA. Where they can struggle is in caring and supporting themselves, so that's something to remind them of, and where you come in. That's if they'll let you.

They make the time to listen, and they care about people's feelings.

Because Earth types make time to listen, it's often assumed they have more time available than they actually do. As result, they will be constantly asked to help and support others with time they don't have. This can lead to stress, exhaustion and the possibility that they will move from supporting into silent sacrifice. That's something you need to be aware of and to take into account when you ask someone with lots of Earth Energy for help and support, as they'll always say yes.

They are inclusive and like to work with other people as part of a team or group.

Earth Energy makes us naturally inclusive and to want everyone to be part of a team, community or group. In fact, those with lots of Earth Energy will do anything to keep people together. They and you need to be aware that sometimes they are trying to hold together something that is way past its sell-by date.

They have a love of food but can have issues around overeating or undereating.

Earth Energy types love to bring people together, and that often involves good food and conversation. It's what they do brilliantly. The digestive system is closely associated with Earth Energy and, as such, Earth types are susceptible to digestive problems, especially when they are bogged down with a problem or don't understand something. That's when they really start to chew things over. The result is that they either can't eat or start to eat more to get rid of and to stop their uncomfortable feelings.

If you're sharing your life with someone with lots of Earth Energy, it's important that you make sure they eat well and that you give them space to talk things through, which is just what they'd do for everyone else.

Living with Metal Energy

Their Big Question is, 'What is missing or incomplete?'

With its constant desire to search for (and share) what's missing or incomplete, Metal Energy can be the most misunderstood of all the energies. This way of being isn't always appreciated in our positive thinking world. Nobody likes someone who brings bad news. And, as a result, people with a lot of Metal Energy can become isolated, misunderstood or devalued. The secret is for us to recognise their brilliance, and for those with a drive from Metal Energy to add in their contribution at the appropriate time and place.

They complete what they start unless their perfectionist side gets in the way.

Dominant Metal types are the ultimate completer-finishers and in the main get things done, which is great for the rest of us. What they need to watch out for is when they take their perfectionist streak too far, and then they can't finish things off because they falsely believe it's not good enough. It's our responsibility to tell them it's good enough, and it is theirs to value and accept the independent evidence. If they don't, they'll waste time and Energy.

They can distance themselves from a situation but can also feel excluded.

Metal Energy gives us an amazing ability to step out of any situation, and from that position to really see what's going on. It's important we value that ability and not perceive it as a lack of connection, care or concern.

They often need to be alone to work something out.

Metal types like to be alone to think things through, so it's important to give them that space.

They like love simplicity and hate waste and inefficiency.

If you want to get something done in the most efficient way with minimal waste, then you're probably going to look for someone with an abundance of Metal Energy. They can, however, sometimes forget the human side of the equation and as a result alienate people in their quest for efficiency. Sometimes reminding them of the value of other people or the cost of alienating them is all that's needed.

They like quality things.

Be prepared to have only the best and perhaps make it last.

They like to know the value of everything.

Sometimes one can assume that those with a lot of Metal Energy are more materialistic than they actually are. Or a bit rude, as they constantly ask how much something costs or what it's worth. It's just part of their desire and need to know the value of everything, and nothing more.

They often like to take measurements and use numbers to do this.

Numbers and measurements are the best way to assess what's there or what's missing. So you'll often find that your Metallic friend has an abnormal obsession about numbers and that, all of a sudden, you're being asked for a number as proof or justification that something is true or not. Or as an expression of something that's really hard to measure:

'On a scale of one to ten, how do you feel about x or y?'

They can feel vulnerable and don't like to be exposed or put on the spot.

Although you wouldn't always know it, those with a Metal-style personality are highly sensitive and really don't like to be exposed. It's almost as if they have a soft exterior, which they protect with a hard and sometimes distant shell.

So don't draw unnecessary attention to them if they've made it clear that they don't want that to happen. It's cruel, unkind and extremely painful for them.

Final Thoughts about the Energies

Tiredness and being in the zone

It's important to mention here that many of the more extreme versions of these behaviours – and the resulting friction – often only appear when we're really tired or in the zone. (Being in the zone is when we're carried away or deeply absorbed by doing what we do most naturally.)

An example of being tired or in the zone patterns between Energy types could be…

When someone with lots of Earth Energy is tired, they often want to talk things through and gain a deeper understanding. Now, this is possibly OK if they're with another Earth type (as they are happy to talk and talk as well), but what if they're with someone with lots of Wood Energy? And they're also tired or in the zone? What would happen then?

If the Wood type is tired they'll feel trapped and want freedom, which may make them snappy or too speedy. Or if they are in the zone of their natural ability they'll constantly come up with ideas and solutions, rather than quietly listen.

Both of these responses cause friction. Someone with Earth Energy isn't looking for solutions or a snappy friend. They just want someone to take the time to listen.

Knowing the energies is no excuse for bad behaviour

It's important here to point out that knowing your Energy doesn't give you an excuse for bad behaviour. We've seen many times that once someone has taken The Vitality Test they can start to explain or blame their bad behaviour on their Energy, rather than being responsible for their responses and interactions with others. Within any of these situations, we have a choice and free will as to how we behave.

One of our intentions for sharing The Vitality Test, and the awareness it gives you, is that it increases the likelihood of you being the best version of yourself and not the worst. That includes how we treat ourselves and others. Our mission is to increase understanding, compassion and kindness in the world, and we want you to enjoy that for yourself and with those around you.

So again, don't use the fact that you now know your Energy as an excuse for bad, indifferent or inappropriate behaviour.

Or, if you know someone else's Energy, don't use that as a reason or means to put them down in some way.

A Shared Curiosity and Conversation

For many people, having a shared conversation about what's happening in terms of their Big Question is a far more powerful and effective way to reduce friction and create flow than a solo process.

So, if you think it would enhance your relationship, please introduce The Vitality Test to the other person. Note that we say INTRODUCE, which isn't the same as forcing them to take it, which will just create or increase friction.

Moving On

We're now going to move on to Part 3 of this book, which covers how to apply and use this information to enhance, enrich and empower any relationship you have through the five relationship keys.

PART 3
The Five Relationship Keys

'Everyone has inside of them a piece of good news. The good news is that you don't know how great you can be! How much you can love! What you can accomplish! And what your potential is!'
—Anne Frank

Within any of our relationships, there is the reality – what we have and where we are – and the potential of what might be. To reach any potential often one has to grow, clear or unlock something, and that's what the five relationship keys are.

They are what we consider to be the five most important things you need to do to unlock or reach the full potential in your relationships.

It's also worth mentioning here that the five relationship keys are also there to help you unlock the ability to end a relationship that is destructive, harmful or damaging in some way. The sad fact is that the best thing that could happen to some of our relationships is that they should end.

The Five Relationship Keys are:

1. The art of keeping flexible and flowing.
2. Finding and strengthening the glue.
3. Sprinkling the glitter.
4. Creating the magic.
5. Kindness, respect and empowerment.

Let's start with the first of our relationship keys: The Art of Keeping Flexible and Flowing, and let's begin to unlock the magnificence within your relationships as we continue through the book.

6

The Magnificent and Elegant Dance

You've gotta dance like there's nobody watching,
love like you'll never be hurt,
Sing like there's nobody listening and
live like it's heaven on earth.
—*William W. Purkey*

Relationship Key 1: The Art of Keeping Flexible and Flowing

In Chapter 2 we explored the nature of flow and what happens to us and our relationships when friction, stagnation and stuckness come to town. In this chapter we're going to explore the art of keeping flexible and all aspects of your relationships flowing.

If you observe the very best relationships around you, you will observe that they have a certain flow to them. There is a flexibility and ease within the relationship in which both people can fully be themselves and coexist in harmony. You'll see that each person flows and adapts to the ever-changing circumstances, like a beautiful, elegant and unfolding dance.

The Power of Awareness

Knowing that we're different and that each of us has a Big Question is not to be underestimated as a powerful way to reduce the causes of friction, stagnation and stuckness and to create more flow and flexibility within our relationships.

Awareness is a powerful force and can in many cases be all you need to maintain a state of flow. If, however you're already in a place of friction, stagnation or stuckness and you need to get some flow going you may need to take action.

Getting Practical and Taking Action

This chapter and the following two chapters take you through a simple and practical process to clear friction and create flow in any relationship.

The Three-Step Process to Clear Friction and Create Flow

Step 1: Get some distance.

Step 2: Observe, reflect and be curious.

Step 3: Choose your solution.

Step 1: Get some distance.

The first step towards creating flow and clearing any friction, stagnation or stuckness that has built up in your relationship or within a current interaction is to get some distance.

The reason we want you to do that is because Step 2 requires you to observe, reflect and be curious. And, as we all know so well, it's almost impossible to do that when you're too close to the situation or in a highly charged emotional state.

So Step 1 is to get some distance.

If you feel confident that you can distance yourself from the situation, move straight on to Step 2. If, however, you'd like some practical advice on how to distance yourself quickly and easily, here are five possible methods for you.

1. Physically take yourself away.

The first, and perhaps the most obvious way, is to physically take yourself away to get that distance.

That could be just stepping out of the situation for a short amount of time by physically moving away from the other person, if that's appropriate. Or, if it's a longer-term stagnation and stuckness, take yourself away for a longer break. Again, I recognise that it may not be possible or appropriate.

2. Stay physically present but step out emotionally.

The second way is to stay physically present but to step out emotionally, to decide to step out of your emotions and into a place where you're going above them or observing them.

This state is easier for some people than others to achieve. I find shifting my sense of awareness to behind my eyes, almost to the centre of my head, allows me to emotionally detach more easily, but that may be just me.

3.   Close your eyes.

Closing your eyes is a great way to detach, especially if you're feeling angry.

Be aware, though, that the very act of closing your eyes in the middle of a row or disagreement could be interpreted as disrespectful or be aggravating, and then there's also the possibility that someone is about to throw something at you. So be mindful of that.

I've found over the years that this technique of closing one's eyes to detach, especially from anger, is really helpful for teaching children who often have anger as a response to friction, stagnation and stuckness.

You do have to teach them to start doing this from a young age in order for them to have this as a tool in their emotional toolbox. There's little point asking a raging teenager, at the height of their distressed state, to close their eyes to deal with anger.

4.   Slow and deepen your breathing.

Consciously deepening and slowing down your breathing or becoming more aware of your breath is an effective way to become more detached and calmer.

5.   Go into peripheral vision.

Often, when we're in a situation that is emotionally charged or intense, we'll move into tunnel vision. We'll start looking straight ahead with a narrow and intense field of vision, and at the same time we'll often become less flexible in mind and spirit.

Try this quick exercise

Pick a spot on a wall in front of you, just above eye level, and stare at it. Fairly quickly, you'll probably start to notice how everything narrows down, goes darker around the edges and intensifies into tunnel vision. You may also notice that your thinking narrows down too. Imagine if you did that in an argument.

The opposite of tunnel vision is peripheral vision, where you open up your vision as wide as it will go, as in this diagram.

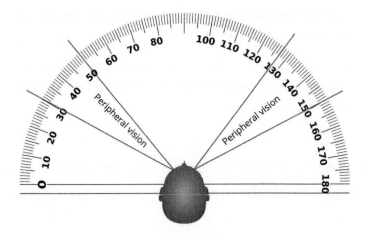

Peripheral vision allows you to have a wider perspective and see more of the picture. This applies to our sight and the situation we're in.

Top Tips for Getting into Peripheral Vision

The easiest way to experience peripheral vision is to do the following:

Put your two index fingers roughly at arm's length (or less) in front of your nose and bring them into focus. Then slowly move each finger out to its respective side. The idea is to keep looking ahead, while trying to keep sight of both fingers as you move them further and further to each side. There will come a point at which you can only just see each of your fingers simultaneously, which is your furthest point of peripheral vision. It's at this point that you'll start to feel more detached.

Normally it takes a little practice to be able to move into peripheral vision at will, so practise getting into that state from time to time.

Now you know how to detach, let's move on to Step 2: observe, reflect and be curious.

7

Things Are Not Always as They Seem

The important thing is not to stop questioning.
Curiosity has its own reason for existing.
—Albert Einstein

Step 2: Observe, Reflect and Be Curious.

Once you're in this place of detachment, which allows you to become less emotional and more objective and open, you're going to move into a place of observation, reflection and curiosity.

To help you with this process, I have broken this down into two main areas of exploration.

1: Observe, Reflect and Be Curious about Yourself

2: Observe, Reflect and Be Curious about Others

It's worth mentioning here that although I have broken this next step into two parts, and written about them extensively, it doesn't have to be a long or drawn-out process.

Often you can have an instant aha moment, such as when they

(or you) might be tired and hungry, or one of you might have some preformed ideas about this situation. All of this can instantly release you or move the situation on, should you choose to let it.

I'd suggest that we all start off by observing, reflecting and being curious about ourselves, as it's always a good idea to take some level of personal responsibility for the situation you're in.

Exploration 1: Observe, Reflect and Be Curious about Yourself

Preformed Thinking, Listening and Responding

To start with, consider if any preformed thinking, listening and responding might be going on for you. Have you already had this conversation in your mind? And is it perhaps playing out the way you thought it would? Or is there a past memory that's being triggered by the conversation, the situation or the other person? How is that fuelling or calming the situation? Observe, reflect and be curious about that.

Another area to consider within the realm of preformed thinking, listening and responding, is to explore the possibility that you've put the person in a box. You've already decided who they are, how they think or some other preformed or expected behaviour.

Look out for inner thoughts or statements something like these:

'That's so like a man (or a woman).'

'I know what this person is like.'

'I knew that they'd say or do that.'

'That's so typical of a butcher, a baker or a candlestick maker.'

For a more in-depth overview of how preformed thinking, listening and responding based around boxes may be playing out in your relationships and life, I recommend that you read *The Story of Boxes, The Good, The Bad and The Ugly: The Secret to Human Liberation, Peace and Happiness*, which is a wonderful book I co-authored with Rúna Magnúsdóttir.

You'll find details here, at *www.fiveinstitute.com*, the Five Institute website.

The Five Energies and the Big Questions

The next thing to explore in terms of yourself is to consider if a Big Question driven by one of the Five Energies might be at play within you.

Here's another reminder of them:

Water: their Big Question is, 'Am I safe or is it safe?'

Wood: their Big Question is, 'Am I free or am I trapped?'

Fire: their Big Question is, 'Am I loved or do I bring joy?'

Earth: their Big Question is, 'Do I understand and am I understood?'

Metal: their Big Question is, 'What is missing or incomplete?'

Be curious, that's all.

If you have a lot of Water Energy in your Vitality Test profile, is your desire or concern about safety being triggered in the relationship or within this interaction?

Perhaps your Wood Energy doesn't like feeling restricted or having its freedom challenged. Or you're being pushed into a corner by the other person and you don't like it.

What if you don't feel loved, valued or appreciated for the joy you bring? How does that make you feel? Fire Energy gives a brilliant sensitivity but can at times make you too sensitive. Be aware of that.

And then there is Earth Energy, with its constant desire to understand and be understood. Perhaps you're reading too much into the situation or this isn't the time to let that Energy have a free rein with constant questions and delving.

Finally, could it be your Metal Energy and a need to search for what's missing, or to say what isn't right? Does your ability to detach and see something from the outside put you at odds with the other person? Or make it hard for them?

As you start to observe, reflect and be curious about yourself, you might see something you need to take responsibility for in the situation or you may need to adjust your position.

Exploration 2: Observe, Reflect and Be Curious About Others

The next part is to observe, reflect and be curious about the other person and what might be happening there. Again, I'd start with exploring whether or not the other person is in a preformed state of thinking, listening or responding. Just be open and curious to that possibility, and that's what you might be seeing or experiencing.

Preformed Thinking, Listening and Responding

I'd suggest you start by asking these five questions about the other person.

1. Have they entered this conversation with something else going on?

Perhaps they are tired, hungry or have something else

happening in their life, which is nothing to do with you or the moment you are in. How does that change things for you?

2. Do they have a prior set of beliefs about you or the situation?

Have they put you in a box? Or do they have an expectation of who you are, or how you are going to respond?

3. Is the conversation or situation a repeat of a previous interaction between you?

Have you both been here before and have they got preformed thinking, listening or responding?

4. Is there something from their past that may be playing out consciously or unconsciously for them?

What history do you know about them? How could that be affecting the interaction?

5. Are there any other reasons why they might have already decided how things will be?

Within any interaction or long-term situation you find yourself in, it's important to be aware that the other person may already be in a preformed state, and that might be influencing them.

The Five Energies and the Big Questions

After you've explored the possibility that preformed thinking, listening and responding might be at play, I'd suggest that you explore whether any of the Big Questions are at play for them too.

Remember, at this stage it's important not to judge. Just be curious. And also remember that none of this needs to take up lots of time. I often assess about preformed thinking, listening and responding and the Big Questions as we're speaking and interacting. With a bit of practice, it can become second nature and almost intuitive.

Here are a few examples of different ways in which each of the Big Question might be showing up in your relationships or the current interaction.

Water Energy and their Big Question:
'Am I or is it safe?'

Whenever you or anyone suggests something new their first response will be about safety or if there are enough resources, such as time, energy or money, etc.

They bring up the past when something goes wrong, especially if the past event was around safety or resources. Although bringing up the past isn't exclusive to Water Energy, it is more common with this Energy.

They indulge in crazy risk-taking or thrill-seeking. This is when someone is testing to try and find the answer to their Big Question about being safe.

Wood Energy and their Big Question:

'Am I free or am I trapped?'

They respond to you in an explosive way, which seems to be disproportionate to the circumstance, especially if you say they can't do something, or you keep pushing them on a subject.

They become overly controlling when they are under stress. A typical Wood Energy response to stress is to feel trapped and out of control, so they start to control what they can.

They make provocative remarks if they feel trapped or bored. They're testing their boundaries to see how much freedom they have.

Fire Energy and their Big Question:

'Am I loved or do I bring joy?'

They look, ask or test for signs of being loved or valued for who they truly are. This could be just seeking love and approval or, in a more extreme form, by having an affair.

They constantly compete with you for someone else's love, attention or approval.

They are highly sensitive when someone says something about them which indicates that the other person doesn't like, love or approve of them.

Earth Energy and their Big Question:

'Do I understand or am I understood?'

They have a tendency to revisit a topic or relive a situation over and over again to try and get some better understanding.

They say with emotion, 'You don't understand me, or what I am saying.' This may be true, but the lack of understanding is clearly causing great pain.

They never ask for any help or support. This form of silently getting on with it is often a test to see if they or their needs are understood by you or others.

Metal Energy and their Big Question:
'What is missing or incomplete?'

They appear to be negative or critical by constantly pointing out what's missing, incomplete or hasn't been done. Wood types can do this too, but often it's done in a more controlling way.

They can have an ongoing struggle with the loss of something or someone, which often shows up as a withdrawal from what they still have. Or they may not show any sign of loss or any emotion. Metal types feel the loss so intensely sometimes they just can't go there.

They are constantly driven by an unstoppable need for perfection or quality.

An Example

Let's pull out a practical example to illustrate the interaction between two people with different energies and how their respective Big Questions might play out.

Jane and Tim have different energies. Jane has lots of Wood Energy and, due to her Big Question, is always concerned about freedom. Tim, on the other hand, has dominant Earth Energy and as a result of his Big Question wants to understand and be understood.

And therein sits the heart of the problem within their

relationship – and the brilliance.

When Jane has an idea and wants to run with it, she is destroyed by Tim and his need to understand and to know every detail. He asks questions like, 'What will happen? How it will work?' For Jane the fact that Tim wants to understand everything ruins Jane's sense of freedom, creativity and spontaneity, and she feels she can't be in the moment or be free to act spontaneously. He holds her back, and that causes friction between them.

For Tim this tension isn't great, either. He wants to explore and enjoy what Jane is thinking about by asking questions and getting more details. For him, the exploration and the understanding are both essential to him and fun, almost as much fun as the actual doing. Plus, it reduces his stress levels about Jane and her flow of new ideas. He loves her and wants to make sure she's going to be OK with what she has planned. But that involves asking questions, most of which Jane doesn't have the answer to, because she's only just thought of the idea.

After a few years of this tension, their relationship is in a bad way. Tim is withdrawn and feels misunderstood, and Jane is angry that he's such a negative force in her life. They've reached a stage when they are now looking out for what they see as each other's negative behaviour to try and prove that their perception of each other is right.

And as for their sex life, that's great. Only kidding. They haven't had sex for about nine months and that's starting to feel normal.

There you have it. Two people who were deeply in love pulled apart and on the road to separation because their Big Questions in life are different and they don't know what to do about those differences.

Remember that knowing the energies is not an excuse for bad behaviour.

It's important to remind ourselves that knowing your Energy does not give you an excuse for bad behaviour. We always have a choice and free will around how we behave.

Improving your skill at spotting the Big Question

Being able to spot when someone is responding to or testing their Big Question is a skill and can take some time to master. The important thing is to be detached (in a compassionate, caring way) and to remain open and wonderfully curious.

Now you've observed, reflected and been curious and have hopefully started to see the other person, yourself or the situation in a new light, it's time to move on to Step 3, which is to choose your solution.

8

Problem? What Problem?

'A problem isn't a real problem till you decide to make it a problem ...
so what's the problem again?'
—Rúna Magnúsdóttir

Sometimes just being aware that you are (or someone else is) just playing out their Big Question, or that some other aspect of their Energy is at play, is often enough to shift everything into a different place, and to create flow and understanding in the relationship or interaction…

As can be the realisation that one of you is coming from a place of preformed thinking, listening or responding, and that may be leading to a lack of flow.

And if that shift hasn't happened yet?

Then I suggest that you move on to the next step, Step 3.

Step 3: Choose Your Solution.

All the possible solutions I am suggesting in Step 3 are designed to reduce tension, move stagnation and create flow in your all your relationships, or the current situation you're in.

Here's a menu of five possible solutions that you can dip into as a solution to the relationship issue you have, and what you've found as a result of observing, reflecting and being curious in Step 2 of our process to create flow and remove any friction, stagnation and stuckness.

Possible Solution 1: Conscious Questions.

Possible Solution 2: Change the energy.

Possible Solution 3: Yielding or challenging.

Possible Solution 4: Forgiving.

Possible Solution 5: Developing your higher self.

The solutions here are the ones I found during my thirty-five years in practice that seem to work the best, but I am sure you'll have your own solutions and ideas too. So, if appropriate, add those into the mix as well. And of course, with these five possible solutions you can apply them all, or just one or two. It's up to you. The important thing is be open to all possibilities.

It's worth noting here that you may not be able to apply your solution there and then. You may have to play a longer game in order to have kind and flowing relationships.

Before we start to look at all the possible solutions I wanted to give you a brief overview of what I call Conscious Questions, which are a powerful and helpful solution for any relationship issue or any situation in life.

After you've got an understanding of what Conscious Questions are, we'll then get back to putting them into action as we continue with Step 3 and choosing a solution.

Conscious Questions

One of the difficulties we have, when we try to change our thinking or behaviour in our relationships, is that much of who we are and how we manifest in the world comes from our unconscious mind. And it's well recognised that trying to change anything in your unconscious mind, or in your unconsciously driven behaviour, is notoriously hard to do. This is where Conscious Questions come in.

A Conscious Question is any question that you ask on purpose, in a mindful or a conscious way, that is designed to get a helpful answer.

A helpful answer would be one that inspires you, empowers you, calms you, relaxes you, excites you or creates a more balanced view of yourself or of others. It could also give you a solution to a problem that you're struggling with or a simple way to move forward.

Conscious Questions have the ability to tap directly into your unconscious mind and, while there, to alter your stored memories, beliefs and perceptions about anything and anyone. Conscious Questions do all that by utilising one of the major functions of the unconscious mind: to answer questions.

The unconscious mind is constantly working away, answering any questions it's asked. And here's the important bit: it only works on answering the question it's been asked, and nothing else. It doesn't try to flip it around or change the question. It just answers the question.

So, if for example, you asked, 'Why is my husband being so annoying?' then your unconscious mind would answer that question and tell you why your husband was being so annoying.

The unconscious mind isn't looking for a balanced view – that's unless you ask it for a balanced view, and then you'd get one.

If, for example, you asked why your husband was sometimes helpful, and also at times annoying, your unconscious mind would tell you why that was true.

So you can consciously construct a question that will give you a more balanced or helpful view of anything you choose to look at, including any difficulties you have in your relationships or how you view the world.

That's what Conscious Questions are, and why they are so powerful.

Conscious Questions, when used properly, are life-changing.

Conscious Questions and the Imagination

Another powerful part of the mind that you can utilise to help you with Conscious Questions is the imagination. The imagination is again activated by questions. But, unlike the unconscious mind, which retrieves information, the imagination creates it.

Whenever you ask a question, the imagination goes to work and answers the exact question it was given. It creates all kinds of images and ideas, which may or may not be a true reflection of reality and which may or may not serve you. So it's vital that you choose a Conscious Question that you consciously design to serve you and others in a positive way that moves you towards the ideal outcome (ideally, for all).

A Conscious Question should be asked with intent, as if you really want the answer and it matters to you. You can just ask it once, or you can ask it a few times in a row.

9

The Power of an Inspired Question

'If you want the right answer — then ask the right question.'
—*Nicholas Haines*

Step 3: Choose Your Solution (continued).

Possible Solution 1: Conscious Questions.

Now we have looked at Conscious Questions and their power, let's explore how to use them to enable you to find a way through any challenges you have within your relationships.

Examples of Conscious Questions and what to expect

A simple, yet powerful Conscious Question to ask – when you've recognised in Step 2 that you're both running different Big Questions – is:

'Why is it important to remember that we're both different?'

Again, this is a Conscious Question and should be asked with intent.

The desired outcome for this question is for your unconscious mind to recognise that we're all different. Often we know this logically and intellectually, but that's not the same as evoking your unconscious mind and your imagination to recognise this and experience the full impact of that realisation.

What can you expect once you've asked that Conscious Question with intent?

With any conscious question, you don't always have to have an answer or answers coming into your head in the form of thoughts, although that can happen. Often what you will experience is a shift in the way you feel about the situation as well as perhaps some new thinking.

It could be that you feel more relaxed or comfortable with whatever's happening. Or you could just have a wider perspective or a more balanced view, and then be able to see both sides of the argument or position.

Action Time

I want you to think of a situation where you and your partner clearly both had a different point of view on something or approached something from a different angle, and perhaps that caused some difficulty, friction or disagreement.

Then ask our question:

'Why is it important to remember that we're both different?'

Look for the shift. Do you feel more open or relaxed? Do you perhaps feel as if it now doesn't matter quite as much, or do you perhaps just have a different view? That's all, and it's enough to experience a shift in your thoughts and feelings and hence the situation at hand.

The next example is when you use a Conscious Question that's designed to give you solutions to a specific problem or to help you find a mutually beneficial compromise.

One situation where this can be very powerful is when you've both reached a state of stagnation or stuckness and you can't see a way forward. Here's an example of a question to ask:

'How can I help this situation?'

This is a powerful question that I really like because it often helps you come up with simple solutions or creative ideas that you hadn't previously thought of. The power of Conscious Questions is that they invoke both the unconscious mind and the imagination in coming up with different feelings and solutions.

Or you might want to find a way to rise above this situation and bring out the best in yourself and the other person. Say you're in an argument or you have both adopted an entrenched position and things are starting to get nasty. In that situation, how could you use Conscious Questions? And what might be a great question?

Personally, I find asking this question works really well: 'What would the highest version of me do now?'

This simple Conscious Question consistently helps me rise above the situation and lets my ego or pain to diminish, allowing the best version of me arrive. If appropriate, you could both ask this question: 'What would the highest version of each of us do right now?'

Sometimes I also ask, just to have the contrasting view and to give me something to move away from, 'What would the lowest version of me do right now?'

I remember I got into a little row with this person who very lightly reversed into my car and then proceeded to get really angry with me. I couldn't understand how he thought I'd hit his car while I was parked or why he was so angry at me. My Wood Energy sense of injustice really wasn't happy.

So I asked myself, 'What would the lowest version of me do in this situation?' I decided I'd be really nice, tell them it was fine, and, when he left his car, I'd let down three of his tyres (knowing it's never a good thing to have three flat tyres at the same time).

Then I asked, 'What would the highest version of me do right now?' I decided I'd probably rise above the situation, not be angry back at him and move on, especially as I have a slightly scruffy car already. And clearly, he was in a bad space to go off like that.

So I calmed the situation down, he left, and I let down three of his tyres.

Not really.

In the end I was a reasonably high version of myself by detaching and not jumping all over the injustice. Quite quickly he ran out of steam and realised that I couldn't have hit his car. This then resulted in him giving me some money for the scrape, which I took.

Action Time

Have a go right now and think of a situation where you didn't appear as your best, or you said something that you might regret now.

Ask the Conscious Question and wait for the answer: 'What would the highest version of me do if I was in that situation again?' It should help for the future and allow you to see more options.

If memories of that event trigger some guilt or discomfort about the past, you can again use a Conscious Question to help with that too. One I like is this: 'Why is the past the past and now is now?'

Don't worry about the logic. Your unconscious knows, and you will start to put the past behind you. To support that question and to recognise that you're a different person from the old version of yourself, you could also ask, 'Why am I constantly growing?'

Conscious Questions and Personal Empowerment

Another powerful use of Conscious Questions is in the area of personal empowerment. One aspect of this is having the ability to rise above any situation you find yourself in. As you may remember from the beginning of the book, we talked about all the challenges we face in our relationships.

Challenge Number 2 was that we don't always have the best relationship with ourselves. This really matters, since feeling good about yourself is one of the cornerstones of having healthy and empowering relationships with others.

To look at this area of personal empowerment, let's go back to the fact that your unconscious mind has to answer any question you ask, and that you also have a brilliant, wonderful and powerful imagination that also has to answer any question you ask – and again, only that question, nothing else.

So, if for example, you asked, 'Why am I so stupid?' then your unconscious mind would answer that question and tell you why you're stupid, and your imagination would join in and start to make up all sorts of rubbish in its attempt to answer that question too.

But what if you were to ask, 'Why am I powerful and yet flexible?' what would happen then?

Your unconscious mind and imagination would tell you exactly why you're powerful and yet flexible, and as a result, you'd feel more powerful and flexible and act that way. And your relationships and you would benefit.

And you can go to **www.consciousquestions.com** if you'd like to know more about Conscious Questions.

10

Recipes for Kindness and Flow

*'If you make decisions based upon people's reactions or
judgments then you make really boring choices.'*
—*Heath Ledger*

The way I like to think of all the five possible solutions is that they
are ingredients in a recipe. You decide how you'd like to improve the
situation or relationship you're in and then select the ingredients
you need to make that dish. As with creating any dish or delicious
feast, much of it comes down to the ingredients you have available,
personal taste and technical ability. Now you've started to upskill
your ability, and have the new ingredient of Conscious Questions,
I think you'll be really cooking within any relationship or situation.

So have fun with the next set of possible solutions, as you create
flow wherever you go.

Possible Solution 2: Change the Energy

Everything around you and every interaction you have is energy.

Quantum mechanics, which is a fundamental theory in physics that examines the smallest particles and energies in nature, has discovered some remarkable things about what actually sits behind our world. One such discovery is the extent to which our thoughts and imaginings change the way the smallest particles and waves behave within us, everyone else and the whole universe ... and, as such, how much we can change a situation just by changing our thinking and how we imagine something to be.

What are your expectations about the relationship or the situation you're in? Do you ever make statements or have thoughts like these? 'They'll never change,' or 'I know how this is going to end,' or 'I'll never meet my ideal partner.'

And do these thoughts somehow have a way of coming true? This could be quantum physics at work in your life and relationships.

First of all, don't get hung up or worried that one negative thought or imagining is going to be disastrous for your relationship, or doom you to some perpetual state of being, just as one moment of being optimistic isn't going to change the situation or the fundamental nature of the other person. It really doesn't work that way, but there are some simple steps you can take.

The quickest and easiest way to change the energy is to follow these three simple steps and ask Conscious Questions as you go.

Steps to Change the Energy

Step 1: Awareness

Step 2: Openness

Step 3: Imagining

Step 1: Awareness

One of the reasons why I walked you though the process of observing, reflecting and being curious was to increase your awareness of what might be really happening within you or the situation. Increased awareness is a powerful tool for changing the energy of something. If you think differently or have a greater appreciation of why something is happening then the energy will change. You might move from a place of blame into a place of compassion, understanding and new possibilities. So, just by becoming more aware, you've already changed the energy.

To help you here, bring in a Conscious Question, one that suits the situation. For example, you could ask, 'Why is it good now that I understand where they are coming from?' And you could follow this up by asking, 'Why does that make it easier?'

Step 2: Openness

The next step is being open to the possibility that things might change. It can be very hard when we're in the middle of an argument or an ongoing situation in a particular relationship to believe that things will ever change or work out well, but they can. Just be open to the possibility, and that they will change, and as a result the energy will change. And so will the outcome.

As Henry Ford said so well, 'Whether you think you can, or you think you can't – you're right.'

Perhaps you could ask the Conscious Question, 'Why is it entirely possible that x will change?'

Step 3: Imagining

Imagining is a powerful tool for changing the energy and moving towards a new possibility. It's why athletes do it before an event and actors use it as a technique to become a different person during their performances.

Here's the process I personally use and have taught countless people over the last thirty-five years:

I start by closing my eyes. I then take a deep, slow breath and start to count backwards from ten to one. Once I've calmed my energy and put myself in a neutral state, I bring the other person or the situation into my mind.

It's worth noting here that we're all very different in this respect to bringing the person or the situation into our mind. Some of us are very visual, others are more auditory, and some of us are more feelings-based. (Personally I'm more auditory and feelings-based. So, although we often talk about visualising someone, I tend to feel and hear them more than seeing them in my mind's eye. It's really a matter of what works for you.)

Once I have the person in my mind, I start to imagine them or the situation improving. It might be that I imagine us laughing or talking in a different way, or me being different. Or I might imagine us talking about how it once was, and celebrating the way we resolved things or the new way of being. And then I might ask some Conscious Questions too. For example, 'Why is it lovely to see, feel and think this? Why am I grateful for that?' I'm just trying to change the energy and the situation for the better.

For you it might be different. You might see a new scene play out like in a film with clear pictures and images and slightly fewer feelings and sounds. And you may have different Conscious Questions.

The secret is this: whichever way it comes, imagine the way you want it to be and ask a conscious question. That will start to change the energy and start to reduce the tension. It will also move stagnation and create flow in your relationship or the current situation you're in.

For further reading on changing energy, I'd suggest you read the book *Spiritual Growth: Being Your Higher Self* by Sanaya Roman. I found Chapter 2 particularly helpful in terms of my relationships and imagining.

Possible Solution 3: Yielding or Challenging

'The greatest victory is that which requires no battle.'
—Sun Tzu, *The Art of War*

When looking for a solution to a relationship difficulty, often there is a point at which you have to decide to yield – to back off, pause or give in – or to challenge and confront the situation. Which of those two options you choose as a solution depends on you, the other person, the space you're in and where you are in the process. So there is no given answer here. But there are some rules or guidelines I tend to follow, which help me make a decision about what to do.

Rule 1: Be Kind
Rule 2: Be Bigger and Stronger
Rule 3: Play a Longer Game

Rule 1: Be Kind

At the Five Institute, we talk about developing a healthy KindSet, which is like having a healthy mindset except it's all about kindness. So, when you're deciding whether to yield or challenge, ask these three questions, which are our KindSet Questions:

Is it kind to me?

Is it kind to others?

Is it kind to the planet?

Somewhere in those answers will be your guide regarding whether you should yield or challenge. If you don't find the answers there, look at Rule 2 and Rule 3.

Rule 2: Be Bigger and Stronger

Somewhere in your decision to either yield or challenge is this aspect of being bigger or stronger. Sometimes it's the bigger, stronger or more aware person who is able to yield. And at other times it takes some strength to challenge and take a stand. So decide if you're going to yield or challenge based on how big you are, and on the strength required to challenge the person or the situation. Sometimes we just don't have it in us, it's not safe, or it's just the wrong time.

Being more aware as a result of observing, reflecting and being curious can really help here, as does a Conscious Question or two. For example, you could ask, 'Why am I bigger and stronger than this?' or 'Why has my past allowed me to rise above this?'

Rule 3: Play a Longer Game

The final rule I apply when deciding whether to yield or challenge is based on time. If you've ever been a parent you know that you learn quickly to pick your battles. Don't go to war over the small stuff. At the same time, don't be such a pushover that the first time you stand your ground it's seen as out of character or that you've suddenly lost it.

We get used to people being the way they are, so it's important not to constantly yield or challenge and then suddenly flip, because that's what you think you should do. The art of kind and flowing relationships is about us being ourselves and having a consistency to our actions and our way of being.

To help you with the long game, perhaps ask these Conscious Questions:

'If I were to look at this from afar, what would I see and do?'

'Why is it important to think beyond this moment and towards the future?'

'Why can I do that well?'

Another aspect you need to be aware of when playing a longer game is that you shouldn't allow stagnation and stuckness to build up in you. There's no point playing a long game if you're just building up a massive store of resentment, frustration and anger within yourself. Storing all that up won't be good for your health or for the relationship if you let it all out in a fit of anger.

Plus, I'm not proposing that, like Don Corleone said in the 1972 film *The Godfather*, 'Revenge is a dish that tastes best when it is cold.'

That isn't what playing a long game is all about.

Possible Solution 4: Forgiveness

Forgiveness as an action can be a dramatic and powerful solution to any friction, stagnation or stuckness in our relationships. Forgiveness changes the energy of everything. It opens up new possibilities, and is often an act of kindness for yourself.

A lack of forgiveness is like taking poison and
waiting for the other person to die.

It's also important to point out that forgiveness is not accepting or agreeing with something or someone. They are two completely and utterly different things. Just by forgiving someone it doesn't mean you're saying what they did was right or acceptable, or that you agree with their actions. It just means you've released something and opened up a new possibility.

Having said that, I know that forgiveness isn't always easy.

Hopefully, though, as you've already explored the Five Energies, and taken Step 2 to observe, reflect and be curious, you'll have started to gain a deeper understanding about the other person and their actions. And in some circumstances forgiving them may be just a little bit easier.

Again, Conscious Questions like the ones below can really help you with your ability to forgive and move onwards:

'Why is it good for me to forgive this person?'

'Why do I still honour my right to be wronged?'

'Why am I able to I forgive someone and not condone their actions?'

Possible Solution 5: Developing Your Higher Self

Developing your higher self is this idea that within you is a higher version of you. Someone who is wiser, kinder, more forgiving, open, aware or perhaps more evolved. Someone who's coming from a higher place of being, or a higher vibrational state. Some people believe, as I do, that we're talking about your higher spiritual self here, and that's fine.

The important thing, regardless of your beliefs or faith, is to hold on to the possibility that there is a higher version of you. And that version of you is better at creating flow in your relationship and naturally prevents friction, stagnation or stuckness developing in the first place.

Below are seven states to avoid and three actions to take to help develop your higher self and to create kind and flowing relationships. Remember that the path to perfection is a winding road and a bumpy track, so don't beat yourself up if you don't meet all these standards all the time.

Your higher self isn't unkind like that, so you shouldn't be either. It's a journey.

Seven States to Avoid

1: Cruelty.

2: Complaining.

3: Judging.

4: Gossiping.

5: Lying.

6: Justification or excuses.

7: Boxed-based thinking, acting or responding.

Three Actions to Take

1: Choose kindness, self-love and care.

2: Meditate often and think the best of someone and yourself.

3: Practise gratitude and forgiveness, and be in a state of active surrender.

Over the last thirty-five years in clinical practice I've found that if you can move away from just some of the seven states and take even the smallest action towards your higher self it dramatically changes your relationships and your whole life.

As I shared in Chapter 9, I find that asking the conscious question, 'What would the highest version of me do here?' is a wonderful and empowering question to ask, as I grow and rise up to meet my higher self in my life and relationships.

Practising the Art of Keeping Flexible and Flowing

Before we end the first of our five relationship keys, the art of keeping flexible and flowing, and move on to the next one – finding and strengthening the glue – it's worth mentioning that, as the title of this book describes, keeping flowing in our relationships is an art.

It takes practice, it is highly personal, and it has a certain creativity to it. However, even if you apply just a small part of what I have described and discussed, your relationships will improve and flow more easily.

Remember, if you need any help with this section, or any part of this book, Please contact us at **www.fiveinstitute.com/contact-us**, the Five Institute website.

Join **www.facebook.com/groups/TheVitalityTest** our Friendly Facebook group.

Or visit **www.nicholas-haines.com**, my personal website.

11

The Art of Holding It All Together

'My soul will find yours.'
—Jude Deveraux

Relationship Key 2: Finding and Strengthening the Glue

The Oxford English Dictionary defines glue as: *a sticky substance used for joining things together*, and that's how I see glue in our relationships. Glue is the substance that binds us together on a temporary or permanent basis.

Glue in our relationships could be anything. Our love, the passion of a common goal, a hobby or a mission, children, a family bond, a shared history or a promise once made.

One of the reasons that glue is so important to have in our relationships is that, as we talked about in Part 1 of this book, everyday life has a tendency of getting in the way of our relationships. It's very hard for most of us to insulate ourselves and our relationships from the activities, stresses and strains of everyday life. Money worries, time pressures and exhaustion all get in the way of our relationships, so we have to have something to hold us together.

Good and Bad Glue

It's important to recognise here that not all glue is good, and some is rather nasty and sticky in an unhealthy way. For example, the only glue that some relationships have holding them together is a fear of being alone. Or the guilt or shame of breaking up. And then in some relationships there is no internal glue at all, just a heap of external pressure from friends, family or society forcing two people to stay together.

Glue in its healthiest form is a wonderful bond that helps holds people together when the going gets tough and the world is trying to pull them apart. It creates a beautiful connection and reason to be as one, but in its most destructive form it is guilt, fear and shame.

The important thing about glue in our relationships is to be aware that it exists in good and bad forms, that you can create more of the good stuff, that it can change over time and, finally, that it shouldn't be taken for granted.

Children as Glue

In many relationships where children are involved, the child or the children can be the central glue that holds a couple together during certain phases of life. Or it could be that children are the force (and the stress) that drives people apart. The important aspect here is that if your children are the only glue in your relationship, there can be an issue when they finally leave home. So it might be worth maintaining or finding some new glue before that happens.

Glue and Time

The glue that holds our relationships together can change over time, and can occasionally slip away without us realising it. As mentioned before, children can hold relationships together only to cause problems when they leave home. The same could also be with a common mission, say to build a business, buy and furnish a home, or create or escape a circumstance. As time moves on and the common desire or goal is reached or forgotten the glue disappears, leaving very little holding people together other than time.

History, time together and shared experiences can be a strong glue that holds many relationships together, and there's nothing wrong with that. However, if you can also have some fresh glue added into the mix then it really makes the relationship and bond stronger and that bit more special.

Fresh glue could be joining a club together or finding a common passion or interest, as well as supporting each other to stretch and grow in different areas and celebrating that achievement together. Generosity and the empowerment of someone you love keep your glue healthy and strong.

Support and Drama Glue

Sometimes, in an unhealthy relationship full of drama and unhappiness, friends can unwittingly act as unhealthy glue that holds people together when in reality they should be apart. If you have enough friends or people willing to listen to you both and all the drama, then you can go on for years and years intending to leave, planning to leave or talking about leaving – and never actually going.

Then there can be the drama of a bad relationship, where the drama, the arguments and the tension around the next disagreement becomes the common glue that binds you together.

Family Glue

We don't choose the family we're born into or the children we're sometimes given, but we can choose the nature of the glue that holds each person together. Taking time to talk, listen and understand each other as well as fostering common interests or creating shared experiences can lead to a strong and powerful bond that lasts a lifetime.

Finding and Strengthening the Glue - An Exercise

Either do this exercise by yourself or with your friend or partner.

Step 1

Brainstorm and try and identify the glue that currently bonds or has historically bonded you together. Remember there is no judgement here, especially as many people begin to realise at this stage there is often less glue than you'd like or expect. That's normal at this stage, and this section is all about finding and strengthening the glue, not judging it.

Step 2

Assess, as best you can, whether the glue you have identified is healthy or not, remembering it can be a mixture of both. Again, there is no judgement, just a healthy and open curiosity.

Perhaps ask these Conscious Questions:

'What is the most magnificent glue we have and enjoy in our relationship?'

'What glue is there in our relationship that is less than healthy and needs dissolving?'

95

Step 3

Once you have identified and assessed the state of your current glue, discuss it. Or, if this is a solo exercise, think about it by yourself. Which glue would you like to strengthen or dissolve? And then in daily life start to pay attention to the glue you want more of.

Within the Hawaiian Huna tradition and in many schools of thought the belief is that energy flows where attention goes, which means that if you focus on something you'll get more of it. So move some of your focus and attention to that glue and watch with positive, open curiosity what starts to happen – because it will.

You might get an unexpected invitation or opportunity to do more of that thing, or you'll start to hear it talked about in conversations and the like.

With the negative glue, all you need to do is ask this Conscious Question or the equivalent:

'Why is it wonderful to live without x or y?'

What will happen then is that as the glue appears, you'll be less drawn or attracted towards it.

Sally and Frank and the Garden Glue

I remember working with a couple many years ago who identified that their common bond or glue was a love of the outside and gardens. They liked nothing better than to be outside and in that world of plants and nature. The interesting thing was that they didn't actually have a garden of their own, just a small concrete slab of a yard at the back of their house, but that didn't stop them strengthening this glue.

Once they identified that was a common bond, they started to focus on what their garden would be like if they had one. They started buying each other magazine subscriptions, reading gardening books together, going to shows, and making new friends as they visited local gardens each time there was an open garden day.

Then the magic happened, and they don't know to this day why they didn't think of it before. They bought a peach tree in a pot and started to train it along a wall at the back of their yard. And then they were given a small apple tree by one of their new friends, and so it started. Before long they were being given all sorts of fruit trees and ornamental bushes and trees for their little patch of yard, and they loved it.

I remember asking if it was a lot of work pruning and tending to all those trees in pots and tubs, and Sally said gleefully, 'Oh, yes, it's lots and lots of work. Frank and I are both busy together from dawn to dusk on most evenings and days we have off. It's lots of work.'

Just under three years later, they proudly brought me their very first peach.

Finding the Glue and the Five Energies

Knowing your Vitality Test profile and that of your partner or friend can be a great way to help you identify or strengthen the glue that bonds you together, as well as making sure that any bad or unhelpful glue isn't forming. And if you've a friendship that appears to have no glue, this will help you find it.

As I shared in Part 2 of this book, any combination of energies can have a happy and healthy relationship. It's just a matter of being kind and understanding each other. If you want to create some more glue in your relationship it can be really helpful to use the energies to find a common bond or interest. The simplest way to do this is to look at your Vitality Test results together and identify the

Energy you have in common, and then explore together the traits, interests and behaviours from that Energy.

And, if you don't have an Energy in common, then discuss what your main Energy gives you an interest in and see if there is an overlap. If required, you'll find an in-depth description of each Energy here, at **www.fiveinstitute.com/full-set on our website.**

Conclusion

The bottom line is that healthy glue is vitally important to each and every one of us, and it sits at the heart of our very best and finest relationships. So find and strengthen the glue. And, if you need help, ask us at **www.facebook.com/groups/TheVitalityTest**, our Facebook group.

12

The Gift of Glitter

'Every time you smile at someone, it is an action of love,
a gift to that person, a beautiful thing.'
—*Mother Teresa*

Relationship Key 3: Sprinkling the Glitter

Glitter in our relationships is that little bit of sparkle that adds something special. It may be a surprise card, a bunch of flowers, a meal out, a romantic getaway, a box of chocolates, a piece of jewellery or a kind and caring note on the pillow.

Glitter is that little extra thing we do for the people who we care about – something special that brings a smile, happiness or some light brightness to our relationships.

Here's a question for you...

'How much glitter do you have in your current closest relationship?' Have a think about that.

And then have a think about what your closest relationships would be like if there was no sparkle. Or is that perhaps what you have?

Adding in the Glitter

It's very easy to forget to add glitter when we're in long-term relationships, especially in our busy and sometimes stressful lives. It happens to most of us at some time or other.

If you have identified that you need to have some more glitter sprinkled in your relationship, the important thing is not to judge or look at what has been, but what you can do right now. What could you do to add a little glitter? And I am not talking about spending lots of money. That isn't what glitter is necessarily about, and can be its downfall, as we'll discuss. Some of the best glitter can be free. It just takes a little imagination and thought.

Perhaps ask the conscious question, 'What could I do for this relationship that would add a bit of sparkle?' Remember, though, that if you've not been sprinkling that glitter around for a while, don't drown your friend or partner with a thousand and one ideas and a ton of sparkles.

Lots of Glitter and no Glue

In some relationships there is an abundance of glitter with constant presents, gifts and treats, which is wonderful, but only if it's not a replacement for glue. Over time our relationships can end up with little or no glue, or perhaps there was never any to start with. If this is the case, a common response is to add more and more glitter to make things appear or feel OK. However, the reality is that glitter doesn't take the place of glue. It's more on the surface.

When glitter is trying to make up for a lack of glue or a meaningful bond, there can be a propensity to overspend or end up with more and more lavish gifts or acts of love. This consistent over-glittering can also happen when there are other emotions at play, such as guilt, a lack of self-worth, or if someone has a lot of Fire Energy and they're craving that sudden hit of gratitude, love or appreciation that results from doing glittery acts. So use your glitter wisely.

Conclusion

Although, as I said earlier, glitter shouldn't be a replacement for deep and meaningful glue in our relationships, it is still a vitally important component to have in our lives. Glitter adds that special spark that is all too easy to lose as time marches on, or as we perhaps start to take our loved ones for granted. So, as you read this, ask yourself, 'When was the last time I sprinkled some glitter on my nearest and dearest and saw that special smile and look of joy?'

13

Abracadabra, Houdini and Hogwarts

I am a great admirer of mystery and magic.
Look at this life … all mystery and magic.
—*Harry Houdini*

Relationship Key 4: Creating the Magic

And now we come to the magic.

Deeply magical moments in our relationships don't tend to come that often, unless we create them. But when they do they can transform everything, and if you hold on to them they can last forever. A magical moment might be when you meet your life partner, your wedding day, the birth of a child, the recovery from a serious illness, an act of deep generosity or a breathtaking view from a mountaintop shared with someone you love. These magical moments are times when we feel differently or have a different or deeply meaningful experience with someone we love.

The Importance of Magic

In many ways keeping flowing and flexible and the glue and the glitter in our relationships are very earthly things. They are often quite practical, day-to-day and normal things that we get on with. Having said that, without them our relationships wouldn't survive or be as wonderful as they are or could be. But they're still earthly.

Magic, on the other hand, has something different about it: a different Energy. Truly magical moments transcend the ordinary and take us somewhere else, somewhere magical, which is why they are so special and important.

Capturing the Magic

One of the challenges with the magic in our relationships is that it appears ... and if we don't capture it then it's gone like a dream. It's not as solid as other moments in time.

So let's just look at that and capture some magic with the help of some Conscious Questions.

Close your eyes, think of someone, take a deep breath in and then ask, 'What is a magical moment I've had with (the person's name)?' And then sit and wait for that memory. Then as you get that – even the slightest sense of it – smile warmly inside and be grateful.

Then ask, 'What is another magical moment I've had with (the person's name)?' And again, wait for it to arrive, smile warmly and be grateful. You can repeat this question as many times as you'd like, until you feel gratitude and warmth for all the magical moments you've shared.

Collective Magic and Being Fully Present in the Moment

Although I said above that deeply magical moments in our relationships don't tend to come that often, on some level they do. We just don't notice them or aren't fully present to them.

Often we only remember the magical moments that have the deepest impact on us, or are more recognised as magical moments, like a child being born or a wedding day. There are, however, many magical moments that pass us by unnoticed because we're not fully present to them, and our relationships are the poorer for that.

Over the next forty-eight hours, when you're with a loved one, try to be very present and conscious in the moment. Look out for what might be happening, where you are, or what you're being shown.

Try to capture a magical moment, and if you're lucky enough to do so, smile warmly again and be grateful together. The more you do that the more you'll notice every one of them, and collectively they'll start to build up in a magical and very special way.

And your relationship will be a million times better for it.

Reliving and Remembering the Magic

The other thing you can do to both recognise and get the full benefit from the magical moments you've shared is to relive and remember them. Looking at photos from a holiday, reminiscing and talking about something that mattered to you both or putting together a scrapbook of a favourite event or time in your life … it all brings back the magic of those moments.

Creating New Magical Moments

As well as reminiscing, being aware and fully present, consciously creating new magical moments in your relationships is an important action too. To do this, all it takes is some awareness that magical moments are important, which hopefully you'll have picked up by now, and some conscious action to create some new ones.

Here's a three-step process I've used with clients over the years.

Step 1. Identify, through inner thought and discussion, what constitutes a magical moment for you both, or for you as an individual.

Step 2. Spend some time together being grateful for those times.

Step 3. Ask yourself this conscious question: 'How could I create more of those?' And then, when it comes to you, take action. Don't let everyday life get in the way.

Conclusion

The bottom line is that the glue holds us together, the glitter adds that fun and sparkle, but as you look back at your life and your relationships it is the magical moments that lift us to somewhere so much more precious – if you can just create or capture them.

14

Rising Up to Meet Yourself

*'For beautiful eyes, look for the good in others; for beautiful
lips, speak only words of kindness; and for poise, walk
with the knowledge that you are never alone.'*
—Audrey Hepburn

Relationship Key 5: Kindness, Respect and Empowerment

The final key to unlocking healthier, happier and more empowering relationships is the fifth key, which is kindness, respect and empowerment, and that's where we are now.

In fact that's where we've always been.

Throughout this book you may have spotted that we have approached the whole central theme of how to create healthier, happier and more empowering relationships through the lens of kindness, respect and empowerment – it's all we've ever been doing.

Flexibility and flow keep both parties happy in a place of mutual respect and empowerment. Healthy glue acts as a loving bond, allowing both freedom and connection. And glitter and magic allow us to feel loved, grateful and appreciated, so once we feel all these things we can do the same for others.

Hopefully you'll have also seen that those three ways of being – kindness, respect and empowerment – have been gently directed towards you and towards others in equal measure. And if that's not been as clear as it should have been I apologise, and let's make amends right now.

Kindness sits at the heart of everything we do here at the Five Institute, and as we share and explore that with our community and fellow like-minded souls, we are always very clear that kindness starts with you. It's not about striving for more and more externally directed random acts of kindness. It's about how we look after ourselves and, in doing so, how spontaneous acts of true kindness appear in an effortless and abundant manner. Plus we start with being internally kind, because in our experience that's where the imbalance often lies.

At the Five Institute we talk about developing a healthy KindSet, which is like a mindset, except that it's all about kindness. And we'd go so far as to say that it's the new mindset.

A healthy KindSet is when you're kind to yourself, to others and to the planet in equal measure and, if possible, all at the same time. Which isn't always easy.

To help with this, and to make sure that your KindSet is best suited to creating healthy, happy and empowering relationships, I'd like you to ask these three Conscious Questions, one after the other, when you're faced with a choice of a difficult situation in life.

'Is this kind to me?'

'Is this kind to others?'

'Is this kind to the planet?'

The more you practise those three questions the more you'll find a way to walk that middle ground, and the more your relationships – with yourself and others – will start to bloom.

And that's where we'll end Part 3 of this book – with a note of kindness.

The End and the Beginning

I hope that you've found Parts 1, 2 and 3 of this book interesting and insightful and, most of all that they help you in all your relationships. Although we've covered a lot of ground, remember (as the title indicates) that having kindness and flow in our relationships is an art rather than an exact science.

So explore and experiment to find your way, and if you need any additional guidance or if you'd like to share your experience, we're here and we'd love to connect.

Make contact with us here: **www.fiveinstitute.com/contact-us**, which is the Five Institute contact page.

Join us at **www.facebook.com/groups/TheVitalityTest**, our Friendly Facebook group.

We also have additional resources here at **www.fiveinstitute.com**, our website. And finally, you can always contact me personally via www.nicholas-haines.com, my own website.

Moving on with the Art of Kind and Flowing Relationships

The final part of this book, Part 4, is perhaps more of a knowledge base or, as I call it, The Artist's Toolbox. Within this part of the book you'll find an exploration of what happens when you mix two energies together in a relationship. I'll explore what works well with each pairing and some of the most common challenges or what to watch out for.

I'd suggest you perhaps read about the pair of energies that each of you has as your most dominant Energy and move on from there. Or leave us at this stage, and start practising and putting into place the art of kind and flowing relationships.

PART 4

The Artist's Toolbox

Relationships are an Art and not a Science

Darkness cannot drive out darkness: only light can do that.
Hate cannot drive out hate: only love can do that.
——Martin Luther King Jr.

The Combination of Energies

In the report that accompanied your Vitality Test profile, and so far in this book, we have looked at each Energy in isolation. In this section we're going to explore the fascinating and crucial subject of how different energies combine and get along with each other – to highlight what goes on in the real world.

In the next section you'll find ten different combinations (pairings) of energies. For each pair of energies there is no significance in respect of which Energy is listed first. So, for example, Water and Fire is the same as Fire and Water.

This combination of energies could be seen in a friendship, a work relationship, between a couple or within the parent/mentor role with a child. And, although we don't directly explore it this way, as a combination of energies within you.

For each combination of energies we'll explore what works well with this pairing and some of the most common challenges or what to watch out for. It's worth emphasising here that all these scenarios are just possibilities, rather than how it has to be. Self-awareness and choice play a big part in whether or not these challenges manifest and appear in the real world.

We suggest that you look at the pair of energies that interests you most, rather than reading them all. As previously, with the individual energies, I've once again focused on the Big Question and a few key traits rather than every aspect of the Energy. What you'll notice as you read through this part of the book is a series of repeating scenarios and patterns around each Big Question and Energy. You'll see repetition again and again.

Once you've started to see those repeating patterns you'll be well on your way to becoming a master of the Five Energies and how they manifest in your relationships and in the world. The magical thing about the Five Energies is that they are very easy to use and put to your advantage once you've seen the pattern. That's the art.

To help you find the combination of energies you're looking for, here's a list with the page number of each combination. Remember, for each pair of energies there is no significance regarding which Energy is listed first. So, for example, Water and Wood is the same as Wood and Water.

Water and Wood Energy as a Combination

The Big Question for Water Energy is:

'Am I safe?' (Or 'Is it safe?' or 'Are we safe?')

The Big Question for Wood Energy is:

'Am I free?' (Or 'Are we free?')

Let's start off our exploration about how these two energies relate to each other by looking at their respective Big Questions:

Water Energy, which is all about safety, and Wood Energy, which is all about freedom.

You'll probably spot quite quickly – or will have experienced – that these two questions can lead to different priorities, concerns and opinions. One side – Water – is saying, 'Let's be safe,' and the other – Wood – is calling for freedom. At first glance this might seem like a problem, but that's not necessarily the case.

That combination of questions can lead to breathtaking brilliance, especially if you bring in the other traits and qualities of these two energies.

Imagine we're looking at a couple, where one person wants freedom or has a new idea (Wood) and the other person (Water) says, 'OK, let's look at the resources we'll need to get there as quickly as possible,' and, 'What's the long-term strategy we'll need to keep that freedom going or for you to have new possibilities?'

And in return, the Wood is mindful that some ideas may be a step too far, but says, 'Thank you,' and, 'What do you need to have to feel safe and secure?'

Although that's a stilted conversation and not how we really talk to each other, I'm sure you get the idea.

Or we could have someone with lots of concerns about future sustainability and possible problems (Water) and the other person (Wood) is able to come up with solutions and ideas that prevent or deal with the pending problems. And then he or she takes it up a level and says, 'Let's look to the future and explore what really matters, so we can look back and say we made a difference.'

Can you imagine that?

On the other hand, let's look at the opposite scenario, where one person (Wood) tests their level of freedom the whole time with absolutely no regard to the fears and concerns of the other person (Water) and interprets everything the other person does or says as a negative wet blanket, swamping and suffocating all their hope and dreams.

Or the Water type translates every idea and stretch for freedom as a badly thought-out plan and a daft dream.

In many cases, the differences that come from each person's Big Question can be dealt with by increasing our awareness and changing our interpretation or meaning of what they are doing or saying, and then adapting our responses to the other person. And, of course, maintaining mutual respect and consideration along the way makes a world of difference.

Having said that, it isn't always easy.

The secret, as we will so often say, is all about awareness and managing our responses (both inner and outer) based on that awareness.

Youngsters, adults, parenting and mentoring

Many of the adult-to-adult positives apply in young and adult relationships as well. So I am just going to highlight a few things to watch out for, to help you gain a deeper understanding of your parenting or mentoring role.

Or, if you're a youngster reading this… this is why your adult can be so daft.

For example, you have a parent who has lots of Water Energy and greater than average focus on the question of safety, and a child with lots of Wood Energy and a drive for freedom and adventure and everything new. They don't make easy bedfellows, and a compromise can be tricky to find.

Or, if you have an adult with lots of Wood Energy, and they want their child or mentee to experience all the new and exciting adventures that life has to offer, that can be difficult for the child as they struggle with their fear or to feel safe as they are thrust into everything the adult wanted to do as a child.

And then you have the situation of having one parent with Wood Energy and another with dominant Water Energy. With that combination there can be very different views on parenting. One will tend to always emphasise safety and the other will tend to be all about adventures, everything new and perhaps some excessive control.

Water and Fire Energy as a Combination

The Big Question for Water Energy is:

'Am I safe?' (Or 'Is it safe?' or' Are we safe?')

The Big Question for Fire Energy is:

'Am I loved or do I bring joy?' (Or 'Is there love?' Or 'How does this connect with others?')

Again, let's start off our exploration about how these two energies relate to each other by looking at their respective Big Questions:

Water Energy types, who are all about safety, and Fire Energy types, with their concern about love, joy, appreciation and connection.

At first glance, you'll see that this Energy combination pair – in terms of their Big Question – seem to fit together well, and they do. There are, however, areas of difference and a few things to be aware of. Let's start with those.

First of all, Fire types, with their question around being loved or appreciated along with their sense of fun and their happy-go-lucky nature, can have a blind spot in terms of resources and consequences. These are two big concerns for Water Energy types.

And the reverse happens too.

Water Energy types, with their drive towards safety and security, and thinking about the long game, can forget to have fun and laughter in the here and now, which Fire Energy types need to keep happy and on song.

So that can be a challenge, and can be an area that may need support for this Energy combination.

The brilliance of this combination of energies is there is a beautiful balance between Water and Fire. Water types can help Fire types make choices around what really matters, and Fire types can bring passion, expansion and connection that allow even the biggest dreams of a Water type to be a reality.

Or, if a Fire type has become overly concerned about what people think of them, then someone with lots of Water Energy can help them remember their past successes and that they are loved, and their bigger purpose, all of which may make their insecurities feel less relevant or more manageable.

Water types can have issues around fear, which can make them play small. Fire types can often enable Water types to feel the fear and do it anyway by showing them the lighter side of life or by connecting them more closely with the true impact of their plans and dreams.

Youngsters, adults, parenting and mentoring

Many of the adult-to-adult positives apply in young and adult relationships as well. So I am just going to highlight a few things to watch for, or to help you gain a deeper understanding of your parenting or mentor role.

Or, if you're a youngster reading this... this is why your adult doesn't always get you.

For example, if a Fire parent wants their teenage child to have fun, to live life to the full and to enjoy what they see as the party time of their life but the Water teenager wants to enjoy life reflecting, studying and exploring the deeper meaning of life by themselves or with one or two close friends ... then that situation can lead to a sense of confusion or disappointment on both sides.

Or perhaps the Fire child wants to be fully in the moment and seeks variety and connection above all, and the Water adult doesn't get why they're not thinking about the longer term and the consequences of their actions ... then that can lead to long-term tensions in the relationship.

Sometimes this issue doesn't arise when the child is young. Often the Water adult puts the lack of consideration about the future and consequences down to the exuberance and naivety of being young. However, the frustration or lack of understanding can then appear in the child's mid to late twenties or when the Water adult has decided that their Fire child should have grown up.

Water and Earth Energy as a Combination

The Big Question for Water Energy is:

'Am I safe?' (Or 'Is it safe?' or 'Are we safe?')

The Big Question for Earth Energy is:

'Do I understand?' (And 'Am I understood?')

Let's start off our exploration about how these two energies relate to each other by looking at their respective traits and Big Questions.

Water types are naturally reflective and often have a studious, thinking side to them. Earth types are similar, with their quest for knowledge and their drive to understand. So that combination can work well.

Earth types also like to think about how everything and everyone will fit together. For Water types that can be an enjoyable academic exercise or point of reflection, so wonderful conversations can be had.

You'll often see someone with lots of Earth Energy building a home, cooking and taking on lots of down-to-earth roles while the Water type works away at saving the world, following academic pursuits or going on fear-inducing adventures, to name just a few of the favourite pastimes of Water types.

You could also have someone with lots of Water Energy, driven by their Big Question around safety, providing a safe and secure environment for their family, neighbourhood or community to thrive and grow in.

Remember that the energies are not gender-specific, so you could have either a man or a woman in either role or people of the same gender.

Where these two energies can become unstuck or start to rub each other up the wrong way is if the person with lots of Earth Energy starts to burn through resources and reserves in their quest to understand.

For example, this can take the form of staying up into the early hours of the morning talking through a scenario or situation to gain a deeper understanding. Or it can manifest as starting a conversation late at night about something they're worrying about, that they have been chewing over throughout the day (or even for several days).

Anyone with lots of Water Energy in their profile will start to be stressed when they start to dip too far into their reserves through lack of sleep. That's unless they are playing out a game to test their own safety and stamina, and then they will allow all sorts of things to happen.

This could also manifest in a working relationship, where too many resources are wasted on working out how things fit together, or by not asking for help, both of which can be an Earth Energy propensity.

It also doesn't work for someone with lots of Earth Energy if someone with lots of Water Energy constantly wants to look at everything from a higher strategic perspective and doesn't ever get down to the hands-on stage and deliver tangible deliverables.

Youngsters, adults, parenting and mentoring

Many of the adult-to-adult positives apply in young and adult relationships as well. So I am just going to highlight a few things to watch out for, or to help you gain a deeper understanding of your parenting or mentor role.

Or, if you're a youngster reading this… this is why you're sometimes not allowed to grow up or it's really hard to fly the nest.

Generally, this Energy combination works really well, in fact too well, and that's where the problem potentially lies. Remember none of what I'm sharing is a given. It's just a potential and what to watch out for.

Let's play out a couple of scenarios with this combination of Energy combinations, starting with an Earth adult and a Water child.

Let's say that the Earth parent has created a home or space that is nourishing, nurturing, warm and above all safe. Why would the Water child with their questions around safety (and also, potential fears) ever want to leave? And why would the Earth parent want their happy home to be broken up? That is, unless they now want the child to start their own family and Earthy life.

On the other hand, let's say that the parent is the one with Water Energy. With their concern for safety, why would they want their home-loving, caring and sensitive child to venture out into the big crazy and scary world? Unless, that is, they want them to fulfil their big purpose.

Water and Metal Energy as a Combination

The Big Question for Water Energy is:

'Am I safe?' (Or 'Is it safe?' or 'Are we safe?')

The Big Question for Metal Energy is:

'What is missing?' (Or 'What is incomplete?')

Let's start with their respective traits and Big Questions.

Water types tend to look towards the past and the future, and normally consider the consequences of things. Metal types are efficient, love to complete the task at hand, and have an incredible ability to step outside the situation or scenario to gain objectivity. These traits can allow this combination to work brilliantly together or have the potential to hit problems.

When they work well together they are a brilliant team, building a secure and stable future through hard work, sticking at it, being efficient and getting the job done. And if it's in the cause of a greater mission, all the better. This greater mission could be to amass as much wealth, power and security as quickly and efficiently as possible, rather than saving the world, although that philanthropic mission often takes over once they have their future secured.

A Metal type can help someone with lots of Water Energy to be more objective around their fears and concerns and help them find the most efficient way to fulfil their purpose and to conserve their resources and build their reserves.

Water types can help someone with lots of Metal Energy to feel more complete (a Metal issue) or to overcome loss, by being a custodian of the past or by seeing a new and meaningful future.

Where this can go off track is if the person with lots of Metal Energy looks for or constantly points out what's missing or incomplete in their relationship or life. Initially, through fear or a desire for security, the other half, with Water Energy, may raise their game or seek to be a better version of themselves. However, that often only goes on for so long … until they start to reflect, feel their inner resources being drained and therefore withdraw from the relationship.

Or, in certain circumstances, the Water Energy person seeks safety and less critical love elsewhere.

Metal types can also struggle with the tendency of a Water type to waste time, Energy and money on excessive insurance against future dangers. This is what can happen when Water Energy types lose their ability to be truly objective. It can also manifest in the opposite fashion, via excessive and/or repeated risk-taking. Both of these are common patterns that can appear when someone with lots of Water Energy gets tired or overworked.

Another area to be aware of is the tendency of both energies to either detach and quit or withdraw to a place of logic and common sense.

Remember, these are possibilities only. They don't take into account our individual values, or the other drivers within the relationship.

Youngsters, adults, parenting and mentoring

Metal parents need to watch the balance between perfection, sharing what's missing or incomplete, and the need of a child – in my view – to be unconditionally loved, encouraged and made to feel safe (Water). In a similar way, Water parents need to be aware that Metal children can be very distant and private, and as such don't always share (or want to share) what's going on – which doesn't mean that they are doing something dangerous or bad.

However, a younger person with lots of Metal Energy with a Water Energy parent or mentor might be advised to share enough so they know you're safe.

Finally, something to be mindful of...

Water and Metal parents or adults can, as a team, sometimes forget to have fun and enough downtime. And they can also forget to create that Earthy environment in the pursuit of their purpose, security and perfection – especially if their children, or those in their care, have a different Vitality Test profile to their own.

Wood and Fire Energy as a Combination

The Big Question for Wood Energy is:

'Am I free?' (Or 'Are we free?')

The Big Question for Fire Energy is:

'Am I loved or do I bring joy?' (Or 'Is there love?' Or 'How does this connect with others?')

Let's start off our exploration about how these two energies relate to each other by looking at their respective Big Questions: Wood Energy types, who are all about freedom, and Fire Energy types, with their concern about love, appreciation and connection.

Let's start out by looking at a few areas of difference and then explore why these two energies work so well together.

When someone with lots of Wood Energy doesn't have a plan they can feel quite stuck or lost, with little focus. This can manifest as being a bit grumpy or irritable, which someone with Fire Energy feels more intensely than other Energy types. Similarly, when they have a plan, they can be superfocused to the exclusion of everything and everyone else, including their Fire friend.

A Fire type can be the ideal companion in both of those scenarios, getting the planless Wood type out and about and connected with the real world, moving, having fun and making sure that the overly fixated Wood type gets some rest and balance.

Wood types can also have a belief that the end justifies the means, which can cause distress to someone with lots of Fire Energy in their profile because that's certainly not a place they come from, especially if you're talking about how you treat people. A Fire type can be the perfect person if the Wood type takes this belief to extremes, because Fire types are brilliant at allowing a Wood type to see the error of their ways with humour and sensitivity.

With their occasional high dramas and emotions, Fire types can find that people with lots of Wood Energy can be wonderful companions, as Wood types love to solve problems. This can wear thin, however, if one drama follows another, or if that Fire Energy sensitivity is taken too far and they don't stand up for themselves (e.g. by letting the Wood Energy person trample over their boundaries, intentionally or not).

Wood types live and breathe new ideas and Fire types love variety too, so these two energies can really get on well and bounce off each other brilliantly.

The challenge can be when the Fire type isn't selective and says yes to everything, and the Wood type never gets anything done because another great idea has come along. The secret for both of these energies is to decide what they really care about and focus on that, excluding all else.

Another brilliant aspect of this combination of Wood and Fire Energy is their ability to support each other with their own personal challenges.

Wood types can at times become very fixed and controlling, and often forget to have fun or see the lighter side of life. This is where a Fire friend comes in with their humour, their outgoing nature and their passionate spirit. In return, someone with lots of Wood Energy can help a Fire type have better boundaries and control and protect them from burning out. This makes for a great combination of energies.

Youngsters, adults, parenting and mentoring

Many of the adult-to-adult positives apply in young and adult relationships as well. So I am just going to highlight a few things to watch out for, or to help you gain a deeper understanding of your parenting or mentoring role.

Or, if you're a youngster reading this... this is why your adult doesn't always get you.

Parenting can be stressful, and when under stress Wood types can be very controlling and sometimes quite snappy. And when they are in a good space, they are often excessively easy-going.

And that inconsistency and unpredictability is a problem for any child or parent/mentor. Which version of your parent or mentor is going to appear at that moment in time? That lack of consistent behaviour is incredibly stressful to a child, whether they know it or not, and even more so to a highly sensitive Fire type. And it's no better if the child also has dominant Wood Energy or has a good percentage of Wood in their profile. Wood types hate injustice and inconsistent behaviour, and angry reactions that don't match the situation are often seen as unjust.

Fire types can also have their own challenges as parents/mentors if they let their own emotions run away with them, which often occur when they are tired.

Welcome to being a parent/mentor.

Wood and Earth Energy as a Combination

The Big Question for Wood Energy is:

'Am I free?' (Or 'Are we free?')

The Big Question for Earth Energy is:

'Do I understand?' (And 'Am I understood?')

Wood and Earth types often get along very well together and most of the time they create a nice balance that suits both parties. Let's explore that, and at the same time look at some of the ups and downs too.

Earth types tend to be practical and down-to-earth people and, as long as they don't get bogged down trying to understand the past, they are very present in the here and now. By contrast, Wood types can be dreamers with their heads in the clouds, thinking about what might be. As a combination, they balance each other out beautifully as long as they both understand each other. The Earth type can be lifted from their day-to-day thoughts or concerns with those dreams and ideas, and the Wood type can be brought to earth to see and enjoy the special moments of what we have now.

Where the relationship doesn't work out quite so well is when the Earth Energy practicality is excessively brought to bear on a new idea, or if the Wood Energy types with their high ideas leave the Earth types to do all the boring day-to-day tasks. Remember that someone with lots of Earth Energy can be prone to sacrifice, so occasionally that side (and imbalance) goes unnoticed, especially if it's compounded by gendered roles or that style of thinking.

Anyone with lots of Wood Energy in their profile is often full of a thousand and one ideas, not all of which get completed. They can also have some challenges around being fixated or obsessed with their latest new idea, and as such don't feed or look after themselves. This can be a point of frustration for an Earth type or seen as a mission and a role. As such, Earth types can really help Wood types keep the show on the road, but this can also be at times an area of difficulty.

Wood types, with their Big Question around freedom, really don't like to be told when to eat or what to eat, especially if they are on a mission. So it can be really difficult for someone with Earth Energy to offer help and food, only to be ignored and perhaps snapped at.

When they are stuck or obsessed, Wood types can become quite irritable and grumpy and at times snappy with those around them, which is very stressful for Earth types, who value harmony and stability above all else.

Wood types don't tend to be good at setting boundaries for themselves but can be brilliant at knowing where they should be for others. As Earth types can be prone to giving too much or have their time stolen, some Wood Energy advice on boundaries is often just what's needed. The same goes for the creative problem-solving that the Wood Energy brings to the party.

Youngsters, adults, parenting and mentoring

Many of the adult-to-adult positives apply in young and adult relationships as well. So I am just going to highlight a few things to watch out for, or to help you gain a deeper understanding of your parenting or mentor role.

Or, if you're a youngster reading this... this is why your adult doesn't always get you.

Wood types can be too controlling and don't like to be controlled, so there can be issues around this area between both generations. This excessive Wood Energy control – or a reaction about being controlled – usually appears when someone is under stress, tired or held back. All these can occur for both the adult and the youngster as part of everyday life.

Wood Energy children won't stand for even a moderate level of adult control and will react with irritability and grumpy and snappy behaviour, or they will shut down and become depressed and withdrawn. The Earth Energy parent/mentor will struggle to understand where that grumpy, irritable or depressed behaviour comes from. Or they'll just become deeply upset that their once happy and harmonious home is now a battlefield.

A Wood Energy parent/mentor commonly alternates between being controlling and being laid-back and relaxed (unless they manage that side of their personality). This mode of behaviour is highly stressful for the Earth Energy youngster, who can't understand the change of mood, nor work out when the volcano is going to erupt. Common Earth responses to this are to become hyper-well-behaved or to withdraw, or to try and gain some personal control by controlling their eating and diet – all of which can lead to more relationship stress and breakdowns.

An Earth Energy parent/mentor can be very annoying for a Wood Energy child, with their desire to talk, to understand and to be part of the child's life.

Wood and Metal Energy as a Combination

The Big Question for Wood Energy is:

'Am I free?' (Or 'Are we free?')

The Big Question for Metal Energy is:

'What is missing?' (Or 'What is incomplete?')

Wood Energy: 'I've got an idea.'

Metal Energy: 'Let me tell you what's wrong with it, and what's missing.'

Metal Energy: 'Something is missing.'

Wood Energy: 'I've got another idea.'

Wood Energy: 'I need to be free.'

Metal Energy: 'When are you going to finish things off?'

Do those six lines totally represent the relationship between Wood and Metal Energy types? No, not completely, but they are a good part of what goes on between them both, in a brilliant way and in a not so good way.

Anyone with lots of Wood Energy in their profile often has a thousand and one ideas running through their head, not all of which are well thought-out or completed (or in some cases, not even capable of being completed). With their brilliance at seeing what's missing and still needs to be done, a Metal Energy type can be a perfect partner in life and business for a Wood type – as long as both Energy types understand each other and where they are coming from.

Metal Energy types, driven by their Big Question, assess any new idea through the lens of what is missing or incomplete (including not fully completed to their very high standards). This judgement is often done in a detached, analytical way, and as a result, they may miss the fact that they're crushing someone's dreams underfoot.

Wood types have a responsibility here: don't give a Metal type something to look at without thinking it through. You'll get what you give, and Metal types take their gifts very seriously. What they perhaps don't realise is that tomorrow you'll have another idea, or even a creative upgrade to your current one.

Metal types can at times struggle with their sense that something is missing. The flood of new ideas, possibilities and dreams from their Woody friend can lift the Metal person's outlook by making them feel that the world is an abundant place. Also, give a problem to someone with Wood Energy and they'll come up with a creative idea, which again is why this combination of energies can work so well.

There are a couple of areas to be aware of, and the first one is about isolation and separation. Metal types often like to unwind with some alone time, and also like to shut themselves off when they have a problem or are trying to complete something, especially if it takes some analysis or their perfectionist streak is at play. Similarly, Wood types can shut themselves off with a new project or when they have a plan. They can become very focused, to the exclusion of everything else.

As such it's really easy for a Metal and Wood partnership to find that they have separate lives, or a gulf has appeared between them, without either party realising it has happened.

And if you then put into the mix the tendency of a Wood type to be stressed and irritable when life gets stuck, and the likely Metal Energy response to withdraw from these high emotions, you have a compounded problem.

The secret is to really understand each other and to make sure that deep moments of connection are maintained, even if that means via your diaries.

Youngsters, adults, parenting and mentoring

Many of the adult-to-adult positives apply in young and adult relationships as well. So I am just going to highlight a few things to watch out for, or to help you gain a deeper understanding of your parenting or mentor role.

Or, if you're a youngster reading this… this is why you're never alone.

Injustice is the most common cause of disharmony between Metal and Wood energies, both in the adult-to-adult relationship and between adult and children. Wood types are incensed by injustice and will take a stand against it, even if it means they will lose out or be harmed in some way.

Metal types can take a more pragmatic and less emotional view on justice. They look more at the facts and figures and less at the human side and, as such, don't necessarily understand the Wood Energy logic (or more to the point, their feelings).

When these two energies are in this place of difference, they actually have a similar response: to either clash or withdraw. Or, more commonly, to clash and then to withdraw. This can lead to an irresolvable impasse, which can last for years or can result in a relationship that never reaches its point of brilliance.

Fire and Earth Energy as a Combination

The Big Question, for Fire Energy is:

'Am I loved or do I bring joy?' (Or 'Is there love?' Or 'How does this connect with others?')

The Big Question for Earth Energy is:

'Do I understand?' (And 'Am I understood?')

Fire and Earth types tend to get along very well together, as they are both very people-centric and care deeply about how anyone with them feels. Let's explore that, and at the same time look at some of the ups and downs too.

Earth types, along with their desire to understand and be understood, have a drive to unify and bring people together. There's nothing they love more than a family or group of people bonding and getting on with each other. Fire types love to laugh, to have fun, to be appreciated and to experience people deeply connected with each other or with their emotions. In that place of bonding, joy and connection is where these two energies will shine and come together.

Another reason that these two energies work well together is that they both value and appreciate talking and good communication, as long as the Fire type remembers to listen, and the Earth type is aware that a deep memory and a long attention span aren't always a Fire Energy's strengths. Plus, long conversations deep into the night aren't sustainable over the long term for Fire types – or that healthy for anyone.

These two energies, as a combination, create amazing gatherings and groups of people, where everyone feels appreciated, valued and special. There can, however, be some challenges with this duo in terms of gatherings.

One such challenge is that the Earth type can be left holding the fort and doing all the work, while their Fiery companion entertains everyone with stories, jokes and perhaps a song. And because Earth types can be prone to silent sacrifice this imbalance goes unnoticed.

Another area of difficulty that can arise is that Fire types don't tend to have a good long-term memory, whereas Earth types can be exceptionally good at remembering every conversation, event and promise. So there can be challenges around promises that aren't kept or a remark by a Fire type that was made in the moment, but is held on to forever by an Earth type who was upset by not being understood or by the resulting family disharmony.

Although both energies tend to wear their emotions on the outside, you don't always see the depth of what is going on within each of them – which can be an issue over the long term. Not wanting to burden their caring companion with their troubles, Fire types can hide their emotions behind a smile and a joke. And not wanting to bring their worries to the party and dampen the mood, Earth types can be prone to quietly chewing them over in silence. So it's important to recognise, for both energies, that what you see or hear on the outside may not be the whole story – or it may even be a cover-up – and some gentle, empathetic probing may well be appreciated and of value to your friend or partner.

Rhythm and routine suit both Earth and Fire types, but perhaps that lifestyle comes more naturally to Earth types, and they can become frustrated with the Fire Energy's love of variety or the thrill of being late or just on time.

Youngsters, adults, parenting and mentoring

Many of the adult-to-adult positives apply in young and adult relationships as well. So I am just going to highlight a few things to watch out for, or to help you gain a deeper understanding in your parenting or mentor role.

Or, if you're a youngster reading this... This is why your adult doesn't always get or understand you.

One of the challenges for an Earth Energy parent or mentor is when their once tremendously loving and affectionate Fiery child turns their attention elsewhere and falls in love with the outside world. Earth types can struggle to understand how someone can change their affections so quickly and can wonder where the love and cuddles have gone. And a Fire child finds it stifling to be asked what time they are going to be in, what they are doing tomorrow, and if they have eaten, washed, or done some routine task.

Or the Fire parent can't understand why their Earth child wants to be at home when they could be out at a party. Having said that, they're often secretly quite pleased that they are at home, especially if there is lots of laughter, love and affection.

Fire and Metal Energy as a Combination

The Big Question for Fire Energy is:

'Am I loved or do I bring joy?' (Or 'Is there love?' Or 'How does this connect with others?')

The Big Question for Metal Energy is:

'What is missing?' (Or 'What is incomplete?')

Let's start our exploration of how these two energies relate to each other and get on by looking at their respective traits and Big Questions.

One of the first considerations between these two energies is the issue of doing what you say in the timescale you promised. Fire types are very passionate, talk a lot, say yes to everything, and often try to fit in too much. As a result they don't always keep their promises or can run late. Metal types, on the other hand, are far more selective in terms of what they take on, get things done, and are very aware and precise about time. So, as a combination, these two energies can struggle and encounter tension and unhappiness in that department.

They are, however, very good at balancing each other out, and Fire types love nothing more than getting the deep and meaningful approval from a Metal type who means what they say and considers the value of everyone and everything. So a Metal type can be great at making a Fire type raise their game and be a better person in those areas. (However, for this to work, the Metal person has to know how to communicate in a way that lands well with the Fire Energy person and doesn't wound them – or at least, not in a harsh, uncaring way.)

In return, someone with lots of Fire Energy will make a Metal type feel more complete and as if their world is more rounded and whole as they bring such warmth, laughter and a world of possibilities right to the front door and into the heart of the home or workplace. The only caveat in that area is that the Fire type needs to be aware that distraction is not appreciated when there are tight deadlines or a need for peace and quiet.

In many cultures over recent years positive thinking has been increasingly regarded as a preferred trait and way of looking at the world, which suits Fire types to the ground as that's a way of thinking that seems to come naturally to them. Metal types, on the other hand, are currently out of fashion with their Big Question of 'What is missing?' or 'What is incomplete?'

Although they go about achieving this in different ways, both Metal and Fire types, in the main, want to be valued and appreciated, so this opinion that positive thinking is a virtue can cause some difficulties between these two energies and how much they are valued externally by others. (Fire types who can learn to focus more and avoid seeking too much external validation find they become more valued and respected over time by Metal types.)

The combination of Metal and Fire types can be the very best at saving and keeping within budget, or the very worst. Normally Metal types, with their desire for minimalism and clear spaces along with their need to prevent waste, nicely control the Fire Energy tendency to be impulsive and their 'I must buy it now' attitude. Where this combination can go wrong is if the Metal type succumbs to the Fire desire to buy and insists on only buying the very best.

That's one expensive and often debt-fuelled combination.

Youngsters, adults, parenting and mentoring

Many of the adult-to-adult positives apply in young and adult relationships as well. So I am just going to highlight a few things to watch out for, or to help you gain a deeper understanding in your parenting or mentor role.

Or, if you're a youngster reading this... this is why your adult doesn't always get you.

For example, there will be tension and stress if a Fire parent wants their teenage child to have fun, to live life to the full and to enjoy what they see as the party time of their life when the Metal teenager is more introspective or perhaps shy and wants to enjoy life studying, working hard and doing a really good job.

Or if the Fire child wants to be fully in the moment and seeks variety and connection above all, and the Metal parent just sees them wasting time with a thousand and one friends with little regard for a job well done, that will also make for a miserable dynamic.

And then there's timekeeping. Fire types are very passionate, say yes to everything, and often try to fit in too much. As a result they don't always keep their promises or can run late. So, if you're a Metal child, just know that your Fire parent is almost certainly going to be running late most of the time and won't get why you're upset.

Conversely, be aware if you're a Metal parent that you could be waiting quite some time outside the school gate or at a prearranged meeting place while your Fire child is laughing with their friends, not even aware of how hideously late they are.

Earth and Metal Energy as a Combination

The Big Question for Earth Energy is:

'Do I understand?' (And 'Am I understood?')

The Big Question for Metal Energy is:

'What is missing?' (Or 'What is incomplete?')

It's always interesting to go into the home of a Metal and Earth Energy couple, to see who's won the battle. It's fascinating to see whether the home is one of minimalist simplicity or a comfortable, homely place bulging full of a thousand and one memories and mementos. Metal types tend to like much less clutter and Earth types tend to like to be surrounded by anything and everything that a home should have. This can be one of the issues that this Energy combination has to grapple with and come to some sort of compromise about.

One saving grace is that Metal types hate waste and will allow a friendly and familiar object to be kept in service if it's still functioning well. And Earth types can enjoy having less if it means that they have more space for family or being together time. So this Energy combination can work very well together.

Another area that these Energy types need to be mindful of is in the area of communication and conversation. There's nothing more that an Earth type likes than to have a conversation during a meal, where they really get to understand something or someone at a deep, deep level. With their search for what's missing, Metal types are wonderful companions at this time, helping to see what's missing, or using their detached objectivity to see an alternative view.

Where there can be a challenge is if the Metal type is under stress, is tired or has to get something finished. Then talking is not something that is going to happen. This is where the value of knowing each Energy comes in so that nothing is seen as personal. It's just Energy types at play.

Generally, Metal types are good with money, but they can get into a pattern of overspending if they support their Earth partner in building a home and insisting that only the best will do. The spending can very quickly get out of hand, much to the annoyance of the Earth type, who would have been quite content with second-hand or home-made. As Metal types like to be valued, this can be tough on them as they think they are only doing what's wanted.

In their search for what's missing, Metal types can find that their Earth friend is exactly what they have been looking for. Earth types have an amazing ability to conjure something out of nothing and are willing to spend as much time as is needed to make their loved one feel whole and part of something bigger. In return, Metal types have an incredible ability and gift to make things simple just when their Earth partner is in a muddle and can't see the wood for the trees. Metal types can also help an Earth type step away, let go, and distance themselves from what's happening.

Metal types can be perfectionists and can, as a result, overwork. This can be frustrating for the Earth type to see their loved one not taking the time to eat properly and becoming more distant and withdrawn as a deadline looms up.

Youngsters, adults, parenting and mentoring

Many of the adult-to-adult positives apply in young and adult relationships as well. So I am just going to highlight a few things to watch out for, or to help you gain a deeper understanding in your parenting or mentor role.

Or, if you're a youngster reading this... this is why your adult doesn't always get you.

Earth parents or mentors can be ideal for a Metal child as long as they are aware that the conversation is probably going to be dictated by the child. Earth types are often very good teachers and mentors, with all the time in the world, so again this suits a parenting role. Again, though, they have to learn to let go and not ask too many questions. Metal parents and mentors of an Earth child need to watch their tendency to be distant at times of trouble: it's just when an Earth child needs to talk. Also, Metal parents and mentors need to watch their natural tendency to point out what's missing or incomplete, as this will really trouble a conscientious Earth Energy child who values fitting in.

About the Author

Nicholas Haines is a kindness ambassador, life architect and the creator of The Vitality Test, as well as an international speaker, author, strategist and teacher in Chinese energetics.

Nick practised for over thirty-five years as a practitioner of Traditional Chinese Medicine after studying in America, China and the UK. As well as co-founding the Nottingham Natural Health Centre and the Northern College of Acupuncture the 1980s, Nick went on to help steer the provision of complementary therapies into one of the most deprived areas of the UK and won a prestigious government award for integrated and complementary healthcare.

Since founding the Five Institute Nick has been engaged by a diverse range of companies and organisations, from leadership teams within large corporations through to NHS hospitals, educational institutes, international governments and the United Nations, where he addresses issues around relationships, cultures, communication, diversity, gender, empowerment and kindness.

He also has a busy practice helping people when they are stuck and can't see a way through, or supporting them to become more than they ever dreamed, and to Feel Good, Show Up and Live Well:

Nick is also the co-creator of the **#NoMoreBoxes Movement**, and co-author with Rúna Magnúsdóttir of the book *The Story of Boxes, The Good, The Bad and The Ugly: The Secret to Human Liberation, Peace and Happiness.*

www.nicholas-haines.com

www.fiveinstitute.com

Twitter: @nickhainesfive

Instagram: @nickhainesfive

Facebook: @nick.haines1

The breezes at dawn have secrets to tell you

Don't go back to sleep!

You must ask for what you really want.

Don't go back to sleep!

People are going back and forth

across the doorsill where the two worlds touch,

The door is round and open

Don't go back to sleep!

Rumi